Flora's Kitchen

Recipes from a New Mexico Family

La Cocina de Flora

Recetas de una Familia de Nuevo Mexico

REGINA ROMERO

TREASURE CHEST BOOKS

ISBN 1887896-10-4

The text of this book is set in Stempel Schneidler.
Edited by Linnea Gentry
Designed by Julie Sullivan
Linocut illustrations by David Danz

Printed in Canada

Treasure Chest Books
P. O. Box 5250
Tucson, AZ 85703-0250
(520) 623-9558

Flora's Kitchen

Recipes from a New Mexico Family

La Cocina de Flora

Recetas de una Familia de Nuevo Mexico

Table of Contents

List of Illustrations

DEDICATION

I dedicate this book to my grandchildren—
Morgan Renée, Jess Giovanni,
and Sage Jon—our family's future.

Melitón Romero and Flora Durán Romero surrounded by their eleven children.
Clockwise from the top: The authors parents, Antonio Arturo Romero and Benina
Bustamante Romero, with three of their children (Lorease, Loriboy, and Marsha) in
1945; Melquiades with Grandma Flora and his daughter Angie; Fernando; Román
during WWII; Andrés (Tito); Dolores; Mary; Lupe; Flora (Lala) with her husband
Mervin Holcomb; Jenny (Juana); Carlotta with her husband Benny.

Chapter 1

Somos Manitos

Grandma Flora with daughter Dolores
(Sister Anthony) and granddaughter
Eleanor Garcia

The recipes in this book were handed down to me and my sisters from our father's mother, Flora Durán Romero. She was a *manita*. Whenever the question of our background and culture came up, we heard, *"Somos manitos."* When I asked my father exactly what that meant, he told me that manito was short for *hermanito* (little brother). Hermanitos, he told me, were the Spanish-speaking people who settled in northern New Mexico some time after Coronado blazed his unholy trail through the area in the sixteenth century. At that time, this region was part of Nueva España (New Spain), marking the northernmost and often isolated frontier of the Spanish empire in the New World. By the time Flora Durán was born, it was the New Mexico Territory, part of the United States.

Grandma Flora (as we most often called her) was born in Old Town Albuquerque in 1886, when the *Plaza Vieja* contained only San Felipe Church, a few commercial buildings, and several homes encircling the dusty square. She was born in an adobe and frame house very close to the church, and as was quite common among New Mexican manitas at the time, she was very involved in the church's activities. She told us many times that when she was a child, she dreamed of becoming a Catholic nun. The Sisters of Charity at the church of San Felipe were her ideal.

Grandma Flora was the youngest of three daughters born to Mariano Durán and Constancia Lovato Durán. Her mother (our great-grandmother) died when Flora was born. I understand that during the Spanish colonial period, it was a common practice for a widower to marry the next sister of his late wife. Hence, shortly after Constancia died, Mariano Durán married her younger sister, Cleofas. That made Flora's Aunt Cleofas also stepmother to her and her two sisters, Carmelita and Constancia. Cleofas and Mariano had several children together, including several sons. The youngest of the

A View of the Church of San Felipe de Neri from the Plaza Vieja in Old Town Albuquerque as it appeared in 1881. (Photo by Ben Wittick, courtesy of Museum of New Mexico #544990)

children born to them was our great-aunt Rose who lived in Old Town until she died in 1992. All of these Durán children seem to have stayed in Albuquerque; in fact, the name is still quite common here and many Duráns are interrelated.

By the time my sisters and I knew her in the 1940s and '50s when we were growing up, Grandma Flora was a typical grandmother. Her husband, our grandfather Melitón Romero, had died many years before and she had never remarried. She always wore her graying hair wrapped into a bun,

and her dark cotton dresses were almost always covered with an apron. She wore the black lace-up shoes that almost everyone's grandma still wore in those days and a pair of wire-rimmed glasses perched on her prominent nose. She was good-natured and kind and always seemed to have time to talk and do special things with her grandchildren, in spite of all the work she did. And, not surprising considering her religious devotion as a child, she remained a deeply religious woman who accepted all that life offered as God's will.

Of all the qualities that her family remembers her for, however, one of the most notable is that Flora was also an indisputable expert as a cook. Even when we were children, we considered food prepared by Grandma Flora to be of gourmet quality. All these years later, after having been exposed to the finest foods of many other cultures, we are even more convinced that Grandma Flora was indeed a gourmet cook and that her recipes are some of the best of the traditional style that is unique to New Mexico. Her secrets were preserved in a collection of recipes, developed over several generations, that had perfected the combination of delicious local ingredients with the occasional items brought from Mexico. But it was not only her own family who considered Grandma Flora a master cook. She was as famous out in the community for her *chile colorado,* her *empanaditas* (turnovers), and her *remedios* (herbal remedies) as my grandfather was for his fierce temper, his physical strength, and his gambling. Her house was always open to family, friends, and neighbors—and it often seemed like she fed them all.

The recipes in this book are Grandma Flora's with a few exceptions. I have collected them to be sure that the wonderful dishes that have warmed and soothed the Romero kids for four generations will be preserved and

enjoyed for years to come. We could not have had our *bautismos* and weddings, *velorios* and First Communion parties, and countless holidays without these delicious concoctions. They have been woven into the fabric of our history, an integral part of our heritage from Grandma Flora and our past that we must not lose. We remember the food as well as the events that occasioned the preparation of these dishes and the lessons taught to us while Grandma prepared and served them.

Grandma Flora as a young woman

Flora had completed the third grade at the Catholic school in Old Town when she was told that she would stay at home thereafter to help care for her younger siblings. She learned all of the customary homemaking skills from her stepmother and her maternal grandmother, whom we always heard referred to as "La Grande."

I've learned much more in the past few years about these *nuevo mexicanos* who called themselves "manitos." They lived in closely knit communities in which family was all important. They were kind and hospitable, but they were also very strong and stern people determined to maintain their traditions. Religion was central to their lives, just as it was to our Grandma Flora.

The food that Grandma prepared so lovingly for all of us was the essence of herself. To me, every dish in these pages is a separate memory of her and of the lessons she tried to teach her *familia* about life. They continue to reinforce in me her belief that both food and life are to be enjoyed.

"Food is my closest cultural tie," I have quipped when feeling self-conscious about my less-than-perfect grasp of Spanish or when I haven't known the correct procedure for some cultural ritual. I confess that I am an acculturated manita-chicana. It is true, however, that although you may take the manita out of New Mexico, you cannot take New Mexico out of the manita. Through this food, I remain forever tied to my grandmother and my people.

A Word About These Recipes

Another interesting aspect to the cultural background of these dishes is that many of them were based on Indian foods, utilizing the chiles, beans, corn, and squashes that were the staples of the Native diet. Hence the techniques for preserving and serving them were very often borrowed from the people that the Spanish immigrants found already farming successfully here in the Río Grande Valley.

When my sisters and I were growing up, written recipes for these foods were simply not available. For example, many of the women in our family knew how to make tortillas, but the recipe was in the head and the hand. I remember asking my mother to show me how to make tortillas, only to be confused by her measurements. She measures in handfuls instead of cups, and our hands are not the same size. After countless failed batches, my sister Marsha and I developed the standardized quantities for the tortilla recipe in this book. All the other measurements have also been converted from "a handful of this" and "a sprinkle of that," so they are now as close as possible to the *comida sabrosa* served by Grandma Flora.

Chapter 2
Mi Casa Es Su Casa

Melitón Romero as a young man

One morning when we were very young, my sister Marsha and I were sitting at our grandmother's kitchen table in Gallup. She had just served a huge breakfast of eggs, chile, fried potatoes, and fresh tortillas dripping with butter to several members of our large extended family who always seemed to show up around mealtime at Grandma's house.

That particular day, I remember asking my grandmother how she had met our grandfather, Melitón. Our Grandpa Romero had died long before we were born, and I was very curious about what he had been like. She smiled and told Marsha and me to come sit on the chairs in front of her stove.

The stove was an old coal and wood type made of cast iron, dark and imposing. But the kitchen walls were a cheerful white enamel which Grandma kept spotlessly clean in spite of the inevitable soot from the stove. There was no greasy soot anywhere in her kitchen, in fact; she even kept the stovepipe leading into the red brick chimney clean. An old enamelware coffeepot that had seen many a campfire waited at the back of the stove, always ready for un *cafecito* for familia or *vecinos* who might drop by. Red chile *ristras*, hand-crocheted potholders, and blue-and-white enamel pans and dishes hung on the walls. A pretty floral oilcloth always covered the claw-footed oak table. And a seasoned *molcajete* sat on the wide kitchen window casing that opened out to the dry dusty yard.

This room was where I asked Grandma how she met our grandfather, after breakfast when she had time for a little relaxation. As we slipped off our shoes, she opened the oven door, lifted one of the top burners, and rearranged the coal embers with an old poker that always hung on the wall behind the stove. She poured coffee for all of us into the blue enameled cups. Marsha's and mine had more cream than coffee and plenty of sugar. We sipped contentedly as our grandmother settled between us, slowly

stirring her coffee, and proceeded to
tell us how she came to marry our
grandfather, Melitón Romero.

"I was only fifteen when I first
saw your grandfather Melitón," she
began in her soft singsong style, typical of manitas. "It was in *el mes de
María* and the plaza was full of people for the procession and the
crowning of the Blessed Mother, the
Fiesta del Mayo. I was with my sisters,
Constancia and Carmelita. We were
allowed to go out only if all three of
us were together. We were all wearing
handmade white dresses that we had
decorated with brightly colored rib-
bons. And, of course, we wore hats."

Marsha and I already knew that

*Gertrudis Rubí Romero, on the left,
with one of her cousins*

our Grandma was a stickler for hats. She had been trying to keep us in
bonnets ever since we were little to prevent us from getting tanned, tans
being not at all fashionable among older ladies in those days.

"We were very excited—talking and laughing and trying to see everything at one time. Of course, we had to walk with our arms linked. And
that was hard to do when you all wanted to be looking at something different! Then we noticed a man watching us as we walked around the
plaza. We walked past him, but I never looked directly at him and he
never spoke to us. But I noticed *que era un hombre muy sólido,* and he wore a

wide-brimmed sombrero." Grandma switched easily from Spanish to English, peering at us over her spectacles. "When we finally sat on a bench in front of the church to rest, he walked up to us and handed me a beautiful box of candy and a bouquet of flowers. He didn't say a word. *Él sonrió y se fue."* She smiled wistfully.

"A few days later," she proceeded after a sip of her coffee, "I learned that your Grandfather Melitón had written a letter to me. He had tried to sneak letters into our house, but they had gotten into my father's hands instead. I heard my father telling La Grande [his mother-in-law] that a man by the name of Melitón Romero had been trying to send secret letters to me. My father inquired about who this man was and then went right away to speak to him. Melitón told my father that he was interested in marrying me. It was as simple as that. My father had already agreed that it would be a good match, because he knew the Romero family. They were a good family, *una familia buena."* At this, Grandma took off her glasses and wiped them on a corner of her apron.

"I had no choice," she continued, "even though I tried to tell my father that I wanted to go into the convent instead. Of course, my father already knew that I wanted to go to the convent, but he only said, *'Él es de una familia buena y eso es todo lo que tienes que saber.'* That's the way it was then— you could not argue with your father. You know your grandfather was older than me, but young girls often married men older than themselves back then."

She smiled and laughed softly. "Your grandfather's parents, Francisco and Gertrudis, came all the way from Concho, Arizona, to our home in Albuquerque to ask for my hand in marriage in the old way."

"How did they travel so far?" I interrupted. "Did they ride in a wagon?"

"Pues sí, mijita, they rode part of the way in a wagon, and they traveled

part of the way on a train. Your grandfather already worked for the railroad at that time. Anyway, they had to come so that they could ask for me in the old way, *a pedir la mano* (to ask for the hand). That was in 1901, and when two people got married, it meant that the two families would be joined. They would become *compadres*. It was very important back then. When the family of the man comes to the home of the girl he would like to marry, they bring a letter that asks for the girl to marry their son. The ceremony is called *el prendorio.*"

"What happened, Grandma? What did they say? What did they do?"

"Well, your grandfather and his parents came to our home in Old Town. After they talked for a while about the weather and little things like that, his father, Francisco, said, 'We wish to meet the girl our son would like to marry.' That was when I came into the room. I was all dressed up in my best dress and I was so nervous. My father introduced me to the Romero family. Your great-grandfather Francisco looked very much like your grandfather, and your great-grandmother Gertrudis was very short. Her hair was braided and wrapped into a coil on her head.

"Later that night I gave your grandfather a beautiful rosary and he gave me a present of satin and silk cloth that had come from Mexico City. We used the cloth to make dresses for my sisters for the wedding. After all that, the prendorio ended with *salvos* and toasts over wine and La Grande's *biscochitos.* It was all very beautiful. But still, when your grandfather and his family left, I went to the chapel at San Felipe Church and prayed to the Blessed Mother. I told her that I could accept that I would not become a nun and marry this man from Concho instead, as long as he was not a drinking man. I prayed that I could accept anything from this man, but that he not be a drinking man."

The interior of San Felipe de Neri Chruch in Old Town as photographed by Ben Wittick in June of 1881. (COURTESY OF MUSEUM OF NEW MEXICO, #15756)

Knowing that our Grandma Flora was a devout Catholic, we were not surprised at what she said and we nodded with understanding. I tried to imagine how she had felt, a fifteen-year-old girl, kneeling in front of the Blessed Mother and praying for a sober husband, even if he was a stranger.

Then my grandmother chuckled, her eyes twinkling mischievously, and said, "You know? The Blessed Mother answered my prayer. Ohhh, yes! You see, your grandfather was everything else but...a drinking man!" She sighed as she took another sip of her coffee and then left us to begin cleaning up the kitchen. I didn't understand what she meant at the time, but I always remembered the story clearly.

Years later, I learned that although Grandfather Melitón had never been a drinking man, he was, as Grandma Flora had said, "everything else but." What she had referred to so mysteriously was the fiery side of our

Grandpa. Over the years, our father told us many stories about this hard-living, hard-gambling man. Perhaps it was Grandpa Melitón's tempestuous life that caused his early death around the age of fifty. But in addition to the turmoil of his father's life, our father also conveyed to us his respect for his father's intelligence, strength, and fierce independence. "It was pretty wild country back in my father's day. Men lived by their wits and their guts," he told us.

Other people who knew Melitón Romero in Concho acknowledge that he was indeed a fierce-tempered, hard-fighting man. My father told us that Melitón despised drunkenness and believed that liquor and drunkards were *"no bueno por nada,"* but that he was a very heavy gambler. I've learned since that heavy gamblers were quite common during that period of New Mexico's history. Don Lorenzo Hubbell, famous for his trading posts on the Navajo Reservation, was a compadre of our great-grandfather Francisco, Melitón's father. Don Lorenzo's wife, Lina Rubí Hubbell, was Melitón's aunt (Gertrudis Rubí Romero's sister). Don Lorenzo was also a teetotaler and, like Melitón, is said to have cut cards for as much as fifty thousand dollars. Finally, after losing a huge amount of money in a poker game, Don Lorenzo quit gambling. But as far as we know, our grandfather did not quit gambling until he had the series of strokes that killed him.

Nevertheless, although he was all these other things, he was never a "drinking man." The reason for this was that as a very young man, he had almost killed someone with his bare hands in a drunken rage. Melitón promised that if the man lived, he would never drink again. The man survived and Melitón kept his promise.

About fifteen years after they were married, around 1916, our grandfather encouraged Grandma Flora to sell her inheritance from her

great-grandfather, Don Miguel Antonio Lovato (for whom my father was named). Flora and her two older sisters had inherited about a thousand acres located in the foothills of the Sandia Mountains. Don Antonio had received that particular land as payment from the Sandia Pueblo Indians for successfully protecting their tribal lands from encroachment by Anglo settlers. We were always told that our Grandpa Melitón scoffed at this stretch of land and was often heard to say, *"¿Quién quiere estas piedras y yerbas? Ni las cabras se las comen."* Translated this means, "Who would want these rocks and weeds? Even the goats won't eat them." The land was sold to a man by the name of Sims.

About that same time our grandfather moved the family to Gallup. Gallup was beginning to thrive as a railroad center and coal mining town,

View of Gallup from the north, taken about 1895, some twenty years before Flora and Melitón moved there. The old downtown is in the distance just right of center.
(COURTESY OF MUSEUM OF NEW MEXICO, #15779)

and Melitón (with his younger brother Andalasio) had purchased a bar and trading post there. My father, Antonio, was only three years old at the time, the first of Melitón and Flora's sons to survive infancy. Three girls preceded him, Carlotta, Juana, and little Flora. Several years later, apparently, the bar was lost in a poker game.

Melitón did many things for a living during those years after Grandma Flora and he were married. The family remembers feast and famine, which testifies to his penchant for gambling. I don't know if the word "adventurer" accurately describes Melitón, but he was definitely a tough sort of guy. He worked as an armed guard on trains that went into Mexico and then back up to New Mexico and Arizona, safeguarding shipments for the traders whose goods traveled over the wide, lonely plains and plateaus of the Southwest. According to my father's youngest sister, Dolores Romero Hinman, Grandpa Melitón sometimes transported prisoners from state to state, traveling as far away as Chicago.

I always thought it was ironic that although Grandpa was such a "tough hombre," he never learned to drive a car, even though he owned one of the first cars in Gallup. My father told us that Grandpa Melitón got so frustrated when he backed his Model T Ford into a ditch, he swore that from then on he would only ride a horse. At the age of nine, my dad had to learn to drive his father's car and became his chauffeur. People who remember those days tell me that it was a comical sight, our intimidatingly substantial grandfather being chauffeured around town and the nearby reservation by a slight little boy. I wish I had a picture of that, but we have very few pictures of Melitón.

Flora and Melitón had thirteen children, of whom eleven survived infancy. They raised their large family in the oldest *hispano* tradition. Each

child was named either for the saint on whose feast day he or she was born or for a respected family member. As already mentioned, my father's *tocayo* (namesake) was Don Antonio, the great-grandfather from whom Flora inherited the Sandia land. When Melitón died in 1932, Flora still had five children at home to raise.

Grandpa was well known in their community, and his funeral was very well attended. The joke persisted for some years that most people came just in case he really hadn't died and found out that they hadn't come to pay their respects. But Grandma Flora seems to have been just as well known for both her cooking and her remedios, the herbal cures that helped to ease the pains of family and surrounding community alike.

Chapter 3

El Hambre Es La Mejor Cocinera

APPETIZERS

The author at about three years old

The Spanish word for appetizers is *aperitivos,* but we never heard that word when we were growing up; we just called these delicious foods *¡sabroso!* The one thing I do remember about them is that they were always HOT. Most of us had to grow into handling the fiery flames of salsa and other appetizers. Some people, like my sister Marsha, were always able to eat these torrid and tasty dishes. One of our fondest memories of childhood is the smell of roasting chile in the early fall. Chile, New Mexico style, has a distinctively tantalizing aroma and taste that demands the attention of all the senses. That's probably why the only appetizers that we remember from childhood all contain chile.

We recommend that you use fresh chile for our grandmother's recipes, available everywhere in New Mexico. Advice for buying and preparing fresh chile is given in our main dish section, Chapter 4. If fresh chile is not available or convenient, then you might choose a frozen or a canned brand. We have found the Baca and Ortega brands acceptable, but fresh is best.

You will need to use gloves to prepare your own chile supply for the season. The preferred hotter varieties can burn your hands for hours afterwards if you neglect to take precautions. Wash your hands thoroughly and often as you handle the chile, and keep your hands away from your eyes. Also be sure to keep small children safely at a distance from your work area.

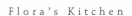

Salsa

Preparing salsa is a highly competitive sport in New Mexico; some people even consider it an art form. Everyone in our family has her or his own special variation of Grandma's salsa. Different salsas are prepared to go with different entrées, to suit different moods, and, as always, to accommodate whatever ingredients are available. Salsa or chile of some kind is a requirement for many manitos at virtually every meal. My dad's brother Fernando always carried a small container of his wife's salsa when he traveled because, to him, breakfast without it was absolutely unthinkable.

The following is a modernized version of the most basic of our recipes. People sometimes ask if they can use fresh tomatoes. The answer is yes, but the consistency will not be like that of a smooth, thick gazpacho, which is the way our family prefers it.

Makes approximately 3 cups

INGREDIENTS:

1 24-ounce can of whole tomatoes
5 green onions (scallions), cut into approximately 1-inch lengths
6 chile güeritos (small yellow), roasted, peeled, and coarsely chopped
2 cloves fresh garlic, chopped fine
salt to taste

DIRECTIONS:

Pour the can of tomatoes into a blender; blend for 5 seconds on medium speed. Add onions, chile, and garlic and blend for 5 more seconds. Add salt to taste.

VARIATIONS:

Many other ingredients can be added to this simple but delicious salsa. For example, some people like to use a teaspoon or two of fresh cilantro or add different kinds of chile, such as "long green," chile pequín,* or jalapeño. Or you may add finely chopped bell pepper, fresh tomato, or even finely chopped celery (after the blending). It's an individual kind of thing.

Pequín is a small red chile that is dried and crumbled and is sold in most grocery stores that handle Mexican food products.

Guacamole

No wedding or baby shower, picnic or party during avocado season would be complete without guacamole. Some people like to add sour cream and other things, but we have always preferred it in its simplest form. We like it best with the most basic ingredients—avocado, chile, garlic, and a little lemon juice to keep it from turning brown.

The secrets to good authentic guacamole are as follows. Use California Haas avocados, the pebbly-skinned kind. Use at least medium hot to very hot chile (the mild chile just gets lost); use very fresh garlic; and blend the lemon juice well so that it does its job but doesn't overpower the other flavors.

Depending on the size of the avocados, this recipe can make between a pint and a half and a quart of guacamole.

INGREDIENTS:

8-10 ripe avocados
1 cup chopped green chile (see Chapter 4)
1 large clove garlic, pressed
1 teaspoon lemon juice
salt to taste

DIRECTIONS:

Peel and pit the avocados. Slice and place in a medium-sized bowl. Mash avocados with a fork, leaving them slightly lumpy. Add the remainder of the ingredients and mix until blended but not perfectly smooth.

Serve as a dip or as an accompaniment to other dishes. This goes well with tacos and tostadas and is essential for taquitos and fajitas.

Nachos

This recipe snuck in on us in the sixties or seventies. Suddenly people were serving cheese-covered chips and putting all kinds of good things on top. It really is not part of our culinary *herencia* from Grandma Flora, but we're sure that she would have enjoyed it and that you will enjoy it, too. It is so easy to do on the spur of the moment or when you need a quick nutritious snack for children or company.

Serves from 8 to 12 people

INGREDIENTS:

1 large bag of large tortilla chips

1 pound longhorn cheese, grated

2 cups refried beans

1 cup finely chopped green chile (see Chapter 4)

1/2 cup thinly sliced jalapeños

1 cup diced tomatoes

sour cream

1/2 cup finely chopped green onion

DIRECTIONS:

Preheat oven to 350 degrees. Spread tortilla chips on a baking sheet and layer evenly with beans and chile. Heat in the oven for 10 minutes, top with grated cheese, return to the oven, and bake for 3 to 5 more minutes. Move chips with a spatula to serving dishes and garnish with jalapeños and tomatoes. You can also drop a dollop of sour cream on top of it all and then decorate it with the chopped green onion.

Quesadillas

This is not so much a recipe as it is a whim. If you have flour tortillas and cheese in your kitchen, you can make quesadillas. These are great for a snack or for a party when garnished with sour cream, quacamole, or salsa.

Warm your griddle or skillet to medium high heat and warm a tortilla lightly on one side and then turn it over. Add grated cheese. (Longhorn, Monterey Jack, or asadero cheese* melt well; and green chile is often used along with the cheese.) Top the melting cheese with another tortilla and turn over again until the cheese inside is completely melted. Slice the quesadilla into wedges with a sharp kitchen knife and serve hot with salsa and refried beans.

*Asadero cheese is a white creamy Mexican cheese that is usually available where Mexican foods are sold.

Chile con Queso

Chile con queso is a dip to be served with corn chips. The best corn chips are freshly fried from corn tortillas. Cut a dozen corn tortillas into eighths and deep fry them one layer at a time in a deep skillet of hot oil until crisp and golden brown. Drain them on paper towels and pat off the excess oil to serve them with the following dip.

INGREDIENTS:

1 pound of grated longhorn cheese

$1/2$ cup of evaporated milk (use skim, if you prefer)

$1/2$ cup of roasted, peeled, and chopped long green chile

2 cloves of garlic, pressed

DIRECTIONS:

Heat the milk in a medium saucepan over medium heat and gradually add the grated cheese, stirring constantly, until all cheese is melted and the mixture is smooth. Lower the heat and add chile and garlic.

We prefer to use longhorn cheese because that is what Grandma Flora always used, but Monterey Jack will work.

Chile Molcajete

We seldom see this dish any more, but it is delicious and simple to make. It's good with beans, tacos, burritos, or just spread alone on a fresh tortilla. A molcajete is a stone pestle and bowl. It looks like a metate, the ancient stone tool used in the Americas for grinding corn and other grains. It's available in specialty shops, but you can also use a blender. If you do use a molcajete, be sure it's treated so that you don't grind flakes of stone from the pestle and bowl into the chile. Try it!

Serves about 8-10 people

INGREDIENTS:

6 large fresh long chile pods that have begun to turn red

$1/2$ tablespoon olive oil

1 teaspoon lemon juice

2 small garlic cloves, minced

$1/2$ teaspoon salt

DIRECTIONS:

Select 6 large uncooked chile pods that have turned a bright red but are still plump and moist. Roast the chile on both sides on a stovetop griddle. Watch the chile constantly. Do not allow them to burn! When the chiles are evenly roasted, remove them from the griddle, place in a dampened kitchen towel, and set aside for several minutes to loosen the flesh from the skin. Then peel it and, using the pestle and rough bowl (the treated molcajete) or the blender, smooth it into a buttery consistency. Blend in the olive oil and add lemon juice, garlic, and salt to taste. Be careful not to oversalt this. It's the flavor of the chile and garlic that you want, and even a little too much salt will overpower it.

Try serving this in the molcajete bowl, even if you don't use the bowl to make the paste. Ring the rim of the bowl with fresh shrimp, large enough to dip into the buttery chile. There's something about the flavor of fresh shrimp with the chile and garlic blend that makes this a very popular cocktail party aperitivo.

Chapter 4

Comida Sin Chile
No Es Comida

MAIN DISHES

The author's sister Marsha as a toddler

People who are not from the Southwest say that our regional food is "spicy," meaning that it is usually hot. To the Native or acculturated people, chile is not so much a spice as it is a staple. There is an old Southwestern expression, *"Comida sin chile, no es comida,"* which means, "Food without chile really isn't food." It's true that most Southwestern food aficionados just cannot eat without some form of chile on their plates. The most favorite chile of all in New Mexico and certainly of my family is the long green kind, cultivated in New Mexico for over three hundred years, often called the Anaheim chile. But there are many varieties available. Some people favor Las Cruces chile; others swear that Hatch chile is best. Hatch varieties do seem to be the hottest. The chile that comes from the farming communities of Los Lunas and Belen, just south of Albuquerque, is also very good.

Some people love the small yellow chile, the *chile güerito.* The güerito is used in salsas and is often cooked with pork as a chile stew. Jalapeños are sometimes used in salsa, in a sandwich, or with a steak, but they seem to be more popular further south, less so here in northern New Mexico.

Pinto beans are another New Mexican staple, and the preparation of beans is definitely an art form. When we were growing up, families always bought beans in hundred-pound sacks. Beans, chile, tortillas, simple stews (called *calditos)*, and a noodle dish (called *fideos)* were the foods most often on our dinner table. We never got tired of these inexpensive and delicious dishes, but on special occasions, such as weddings and other celebrations, we would have some of the other dishes included in this book, like *enchiladas* or *carne adovada.*

Homemade tortillas—*pan de los manitos*—is another art form from the kitchen. Our own mother's fingers seemed to fly as she expertly rolled and

flipped tortillas to round perfection and cooked them to a flawless brown on a hot cast-iron griddle. Manita homemakers had to become expert at this enviable skill to prepare the daily tortillas for their families. They had to be prepared very quickly—and they had to be good. Reputations were and still are made by being able to make good tortillas. We have had some contenders to the Throne of Tortilladom in our family, and my sister Marsha is one of them. But Grandma was the indisputable Queen of Tortillas, we all agree. (See Chapter 6 for our tortilla recipe.)

Chile

When we were children, we knew the summer was over when the chile crop was ready to be picked, roasted, and dried. The fragrance of roasting green chiles was everywhere in the early fall. Ristras of reddening chiles began to appear under the eaves of porches, both as adornment and as assurance that we would have our beloved chile colorado to warm us through the cold winter to come.

Our sister Lorease remembers that the farms of our many relatives were strung like beads along the Río Grande. They all grew chile. Grandma Flora's family got their supply of chile from the farms of relatives when she was growing up, some of which were located in what is now Albuquerque's country club area. Later, when Grandma and Grandpa moved to Gallup and the Navajo Reservation, excursions to those same farms to buy chile for the winter were common in late summer and early fall. Sometimes chile could be purchased from farmers who brought their crops into the more arid areas of New Mexico where chiles were difficult to grow. Our Aunt Dolores, Grandma Flora's youngest child, has lived in Seattle for many years but still regularly travels back to New Mexico for her annual chile supply.

If you are a novice cook of New Mexican foods, you may never have roasted fresh green chile, so we have included directions for roasting it here. Any kind of chile peppers can be roasted and frozen in this same way.

SELECTING CHILE

If you would like to prepare an entire sack or more for freezing, you should begin to look for your chile in the very late summer or early fall. Most real aficionados prefer the crop that comes in September over the August harvest. However, I doubt that the date of harvest is as important as knowing your *chilero*, some of whom just seem to have a knack for selecting chile that is hot and tasty, or buying from proven sources of "the real thing."

I don't know if the heat of a chile has to do with anything visible, such as the size of the fleshy spine inside the pod as our father speculated, but the heat that a batch of chile contains is certainly indicated by its fragrance. Just smelling very hot chile can make you sneeze. Growing conditions also affect the heat of the chile.

Some years back, Professor Roy Nakayama at New Mexico State University in Las Cruces devised a scale to gauge the heat of different varieties of chiles. On his scale, the mild Anaheims and New Mexico No. 6 varieties clock in at #1, containing the least amount of the capsaicin ingredient (which gives peppers their fire), the Sandia variety rates a #5, and the jalapeño rates a #7. The chile with the most capsaicin (the hottest) on the Nakayama scale is the Bahamian (and presumably other habanero varieties) which rates a #10.

Another way to test chile for flavor and heat is simply to taste a few of the pods from the batch you are considering. Take a small bite and consider

the flavor as well as the heat. Take your time. It's worth the effort, perhaps like selecting grapes for fine wine.

There are no guarantees that any of these methods will work without fail, but after a few years of getting to know the region and the merchants, a real chile addict can find just the right bite and flavor his or her addiction requires. We have a friend whose chile selection techniques are so sophisticated that he labels not only the degree of heat of a specific batch, but also uses terms to describe the flavors, such as deep, sassy, playful, and majestic.

ROASTING CHILE

When you select your chiles, you may choose to have them roasted in the big metal baskets operated by many merchants. A butane torch roasts the contents fairly evenly as the pods are tossed around in the basket. There is an added cost for the service, but it really is a convenience. And even if the chile loses some of its flavor, as some chile connoisseurs contend, it's still better than buying frozen or canned and certainly more economical. Real chile addicts usually opt to roast their own green chile and consider using a butane torch a sacrilege.

You may want to try roasting just a few chile pods from your produce market to see if you can handle it, or you could share a bag with a friend and do the work together for a first effort. Roasting the chile will either be an assembly line family chore or one heck of a job for one person. Most people who roast their own say it's worth all the work.

The trick to roasting a whole sack of chile is in organization. Analyze your roasting capacity and your work space. Some people use barbecue grills, gas or charcoal, because the kitchen gets so hot; but if a hot kitchen

is no problem, you may want to use your oven. The chile must be roasted on very hot coals or in a very hot oven. Line your grill or oven with aluminum foil before you begin, as the process can be messy. You will need a clear area of counter space to peel the chile once it has been roasted and moistened. Have containers, such as plastic freezer bags in the proper size for your storage needs, and several dampened kitchen towels ready. Keep in mind the number of people you will be serving with each dish and group the roasted chiles accordingly.

It is essential that whoever does the roasting be very alert so that he or she doesn't over-roast the chile. Lay the chile pods on the oven rack or grill and watch them closely. Usually an average-sized chile pod takes three or four minutes to roast on each side, depending on the freshness of the chile. As the pod begins to blister and pop, turn them carefully to roast evenly (using long-handled tongs or a cooking fork). Then remove them and place in a dampened towel. Wrap them in the towels in groups and set aside for at least 20 minutes, letting the dampness loosen the skin from the flesh.

The chile can be peeled and seeded immediately after the skin loosens up and then placed into the containers (one-cup containers work well) to be frozen. Some people just remove the stems and freeze the chile immediately, waiting to peel it when the packages have been thawed for use.

Remember to be careful when roasting chile and wear plastic gloves to protect your hands. Many times we've been sorry that we didn't remember to put on gloves and suffered from the pain of too much chile on our skin.

Even before the convenience of freezers, New Mexicans were able to preserve their famous green chile for the winter. Grandma Flora preserved hers by slicing the pods lengthwise, cleaning out the seeds, and drying them on white towels spread out in the open sunlight. She was sure to

turn the chile regularly so it dried evenly. (This simple method won't work in humid climates, however.) Some families jarred it like any other seasonal produce, but we don't remember Grandma Flora preserving chile that way. She did preserve all other fruits or vegetables that she could get, usually from the farms of relatives along the river or from the Pueblo farmers who came into town to sell their surplus crop.

Comida Sin Chile No Es Comida

Grandpa Melitón was a massive man. He wore a size 8 3/4 hat. Whenever Grandma Flora went to buy his customary black ten-gallon hat, the storekeeper would always joke, *"Es un sombrero para un toro."* It was true. My dad always said that Grandpa Melitón was built like a bull and had *un apetito grande.* In spite of his big appetite, however, Melitón was very particular about how his food was prepared. Like many of the manito oldtimers, he would eat only certain things prepared in particular ways. But chile was always the main ingredient in his diet, usually served with beans cooked in just the right way and, of course, fresh tortillas or big fluffy biscuits. Contemporary New Mexicans often expect to have sopaipillas with every "New Mexican" dinner, but Grandma served sopaipillas only with the more special sort of meals.

Grandma Flora served Grandpa Melitón's meals in the old way. She would fill his plate and then stand behind his chair to be ready to provide anything else he might want. It seems unfair to us now, but it was the custom then.

This recipe for green chile was Grandpa Melitón's favorite, to eat with or without beans and tortillas. The hotter it was, the better he liked it.

Chile Verde

Approximately 6 servings

INGREDIENTS:

6 center-cut pork chops or 1 small round steak

2 tablespoons cooking oil

2 cups chopped green chile (Chile güerito is an interesting variation, but you
   must be an intrepid chile eater, as the güerito is usually quite hot.)

3 cloves fresh minced garlic

1 tablespoon corn starch

2 cups water

1 teaspoon salt

DIRECTIONS:

Cut the meat into small bite-sized pieces. Heat the oil on medium heat in a
large skillet and add the meat. Stir until well cooked. Add the chile and garlic,
blending them with the meat. Add the corn starch and mix until well
blended. Pour in the water, add the salt, and mix well. Reduce the heat and
simmer for 30 minutes.

Green Chile Caldo

When my father was a very young man he served in the Civilian
Conservation Corps, fighting forest fires in Oregon. While fighting one particularly bad fire, they were cut off from their food supply for ten days. All
that was available were cases of fresh lettuce and canned peanut butter. He
ate the lettuce spread with peanut butter because he was so hungry, but all
he could think of was green chile stew and fresh tortillas. And it is indeed
one of the best dishes that New Mexico has to offer.

We could count on having the following dish a few times a week in the early fall, soon after the chile crop had been gathered and roasted. All that was needed to serve it were bowls and fresh tortillas, torn to bite-sized pieces and folded to scoop up this caldo sabroso. The chile verde recipe on the next page is a sauce that the most diehard New Mexico food fan might have as a main course, but this version with potatoes added is a heartier entrée.

Serves 6

INGREDIENTS:

1/4 cup cooking oil

1 medium round steak, cut into small bite-sized pieces (Sometimes we used pork instead of beef, but Grandma preferred pork for the chile verde and the chile colorado.)

6 large potatoes, cut into small bite-sized pieces

2 cups chopped green chile

1 large or 2 small cloves of garlic, pressed

1/4 small onion, cut into small crescents

2 tablespoons flour

1 quart water

salt to taste

DIRECTIONS:

Heat the oil in a Dutch oven or skillet on low heat. Sauté the onion and then move it to the side of the skillet. Immediately add the potatoes and round steak. Turn the heat up to medium to cook the meat and potatoes, stirring frequently, for about 20 minutes. Add the green chile and garlic and also blend in the onions. Mix the flour with a little water and then add it into the mixture, stirring it until brown. Add the water and salt and continue to cook for 30 minutes more. Turn off the burner and remove the Dutch oven from the stove. Like any stew, the caldo is better if it sits for a few minutes before serving.

Chile Colorado

No respectable manito family celebration would be complete without chile colorado, the red chile sauce made from fully ripened pods. Nor would it be Christmas without tamales made with good red chile. Posole served without red chile would be pale and boring. Even Thanksgiving requires thick red chile, instead of gravy, to cover the mashed potatoes. The texture, degree of heat, and flavor may vary, but the ideal in my family was that the chile be moderate to very hot, rather thick in texture, and undiluted by thickeners (such as flour). The chile colorado made by my sister Dolly's husband, Victor García, is the closest we've ever found to Grandma Flora's chile. After watching him prepare it numerous times, Marsha and I were finally able to replicate it.

Some people boil the chile and then blend the pods with fresh water, but boiling the chile reduces too much of the flavor. Also, the sauce will be more flavorful if the water used for soaking is also used to blend the chile. After learning to prepare chile colorado this way, my daughter, Tracy, proclaims this recipe to be easy. It is *muy fácil.*

Serves 8

INGREDIENTS:
20 dried red chile pods
8 center cut pork chops
4 large, minced cloves of garlic
1 tablespoon cooking oil (Corn oil is better than olive oil in this instance.)
4 cups water

DIRECTIONS:

Wash the red chile pods carefully, snap off the stems, and shake out the seeds. It's convenient to do this outside or carefully into a waste basket, as it can be messy. Next fill a large Dutch oven or soup pot with very hot tap water that barely covers the chile pods. (It's better to use less water than too much.) Set the pot aside and allow it to soak for at least 1 hour (2 hours is better), stirring the pods occasionally to be sure they soften evenly. Place pods and about 2 or 3 cups of the water used to soak them, depending on how thick you want your chile, into a blender and blend on high speed for 4 or 5 minutes. Grandma Flora had a homemade sieve to strain out the dried skin—what in Spanish is called *el pellejo*. To produce this smoother and more digestible chile sauce, you must strain the blended chile thoroughly through a food sieve. It's more work, but it's worth it if you have the time.

Cut the pork chops into small, bite-sized pieces. Heat the oil in a large Dutch oven or skillet. Sauté the garlic, move it to the side of the pot, and then brown the meat evenly. Mix the garlic into the browned meat and then pour in the blended chile. Bring it to a simmer and let the mixture cook for a half hour.

Carne Adovada

Adovada is a delicacy, served by the best manita cooks for special occasions. It isn't difficult to prepare, but it takes at least 24 hours because it has to be marinated. It should be very tender, and the flavor of the chile and garlic must permeate the meat.

Serves 6

INGREDIENTS:

3 or 4 pounds lean pork roast, cut into 1/2-inch slices across grain (Ask your

butcher to do the slicing for you so that it will be reasonably even.)

6 cups of red chile sauce (Don't strain out all of the pellejo from this batch of
red chile—leave in some of the seeds and peel for effect.)

4-6 large cloves fresh garlic, sliced into quarters lengthwise

salt to taste

DIRECTIONS:

Pierce the sliced meat evenly with a fork to allow for maximum absorption of
the marinade. Place it in a marinating container or large roasting pan and
cover with red chile. Place the garlic cloves around the edges of the pan so
that they can be removed easily later.

Marinate the meat in the refrigerator overnight. Then place it in a baking
dish and cover and bake in a 325-degree oven for 1 1/2 hours. Just before serving, broil it in a preheated broiler as far away from the flame as your broiler
will allow, uncovered, for just a few minutes to crisp the top. Serve immediately. It can also be crisped by frying the servings in a hot skillet sprayed with
a little Pam to keep the meat from sticking. Servings should be moist but not
dripping.

Serve with beans, a fresh green salad, and fresh tortillas. We used to serve
carne adovada with *chicos* (a side dish made from sweet, dried corn kernels).
We also used to cook chicos in the beans, simmering and plumping up in the
water just as the beans did.

Enchiladas

In our family, enchiladas were and still are the most favorite meal for
special occasions, such as birthdays, graduations, and First Communions.
However, Grandma Flora didn't serve them nearly as often, perhaps
because making corn tortillas took so much time. By the time we were
growing up in the fifties and sixties, our mother bought corn tortillas from
a tiny shop in the home of a family named Fernandez.

I remember that Grandma Flora sometimes made red chile enchiladas on Saturday afternoons in the summer. Her old adobe house in Gallup (which later became our house) had a long room used as a dining room, off the kitchen. A small wood-framed window in the thick adobe wall created a breeze when open that blew over the long wooden dining table and right through the kitchen. It was always comfortably cool in that room, even on the hottest summer days.

I remember waiting very patiently for my stack of two or three enchiladas. We all had to wait our turn while Grandma fried each tortilla and then dropped it into a skillet of thick red chile filled with small chunks of pork or round steak. (Grandma's chile always contained meat, except during Lent or on Fridays.) She then stacked the tortillas with layers of grated cheese and onion between them and an extra generous sprinkle of cheese on top. She always asked, *"¿Cuántos huevos quieres?"* One egg was always enough for me.

Our casita was a modest little place; but on days like that it was wonderful, sitting at the table eating Grandma's red chile enchiladas with lettuce, tomatoes, and a fried egg on top, with the best iced tea I have ever tasted and the light summer breeze cooling us off.

Serves 4 (Double the recipe for 8)

INGREDIENTS:

1 dozen corn tortillas
1 quart green or red chile
1 pound grated longhorn cheese
1 medium onion, chopped very fine
1 head iceberg lettuce washed, drained, dried, and shredded
2 medium fresh tomatoes, chopped small but not fine

DIRECTIONS:

Serving enchiladas flat is more difficult than rolling or layering tortillas into a casserole, but it is the way they were always served back then and is the way we prefer them today.

First wash, drain, and shred the lettuce. Then chop the tomatoes and onions and grate the cheese and set them all aside. The chile should be kept warm on the stove to ladle over each tortilla after it's fried.

Fry the tortillas in a skillet in hot oil (to soften) and place them on paper towels to remove the excess oil. After the tortillas are dried, place them on oven-safe plates one at a time and ladle approximately 1/2 cup of the chile sauce over each tortilla. Top the chile with as much cheese and onions as you prefer. (Approximately 1 tablespoon of cheese and 1 teaspoon of onions are a good start.) Repeat the procedure, alternately stacking three tortillas with the chile, cheese, and onions.

When each plate has been prepared, place them in a very low oven to melt the cheese and keep the enchiladas warm until ready to serve. When ready to eat, top each dish with shredded lettuce and chopped tomatoes. Serve with fresh or refried beans and Spanish rice.

Rellenos Faciles (Easy Rellenos)

Making *chiles rellenos* is a very tricky process. I remember having them only once in a while, usually when the chile was being harvested and prepared for roasting or drying. We always picked the largest and straightest chiles for making rellenos, as they were the easiest to use. Grandma used a skillet full of lard to fry the rellenos and longhorn cheese to stuff them. Although her original recipe is delicious, my family now prefers them prepared a bit differently. The following recipe creates a dish that has much of the traditional flavor but is a lot easier to prepare and contains far less fat.

Makes an 8-inch pie

INGREDIENTS:

6-8 large, whole green chiles, roasted and peeled

4 eggs

2 tablespoons buttermilk

$1/2$ teaspoon salt

$1/4$ pound grated asadero cheese

$1/4$ cup finely sliced green onion

2 tablespoons sun-dried tomatoes

DIRECTIONS:

Preheat oven to 325 degrees. Grease an 8-inch pie pan. Slice the chile pods lengthwise and arrange on the bottom of the pie pan to form a chile "crust." Use an electric mixer to blend the eggs slightly before adding the milk and salt. Pour the mixture into the chile crust. Sprinkle the grated cheese over the egg mixture and then top with the green onion and the sun-dried tomatoes.

Bake at 325 degrees for 25 minutes. Check for doneness by inserting a knife in the center of the pie to see if the egg is set. Rellenos Faciles is perfect with a fresh green salad and fresh tortillas.

Semi-Traditional Chiles Rellenos

I can't justify the real deep frying required for traditional rellenos anymore, because too much fat soaks into the egg batter. So I make this "semi-traditional" variety when I'm in the mood for old-fashioned rellenos. They're as crispy as a quick dip in the frying pan will provide. The trick to fast dipping is to dry the chiles well enough so that the batter will stick to them.

Serves 6

INGREDIENTS:

12 long green chiles, roasted and peeled but with the stems in place
  (Pat off excess liquid from the outside of the pods.)
3/4 pound of longhorn cheese, cut into one-ounce sticks
4 eggs, separated
2 tablespoons flour
1/2 teaspoon salt
unsaturated oil for frying

DIRECTIONS:

Spray or oil a 91/2-inch glass baking dish. Heat oven to 300 degrees.

Carefully slice about an inch lengthwise into each chile just below the stem. Insert a stick of cheese into each chile and place the pods into a shallow pan, large enough to hold all 12 chiles. Place the greased glass baking pan into the oven to heat it slightly before putting the battered chiles into it.

Beat the egg whites in a medium-sized mixing bowl on high speed until stiff. Add the yolks and then blend in the flour and salt. Pour the batter over the chiles, carefully turning the chiles to coat evenly. (Leave the stems intact.) Heat enough oil in a large frying pan to cover the chiles. Meanwhile, carefully remove the baking dish from the oven and set it on a heat-safe area next to the frying pan.

Using a long slotted spatula, dip each relleno into the hot oil just long enough to cook the egg batter and then transfer it into the heated baking dish. When all the rellenos are in the baking dish, bake them in the preheated oven for 25 minutes. Rellenos go well with the old-fashioned favorites: *quelites* and beans, Spanish rice, and fresh sliced tomatoes. (See Chapter 5.)

New Mexico Quiche

French quiches were not in vogue in Grandma Flora's day, but we know that she would have approved of this nuevo mexicano version.

Makes a standard 8-inch pie

INGREDIENTS:

your favorite pie crust

4 ounces grated asadero cheese

3 eggs, beaten

1/2 pint cream (or substitute evaporated milk, if you prefer)

4 fresh green chiles, chopped (1 small can, if fresh is not available)

6 thin slices of fresh white onion, separated into rings

6 cooked and crumbled bacon strips

DIRECTIONS:

Preheat the oven to 350 degrees. Fit the unbaked pie crust into an 8-inch pie pan. Spread the grated cheese evenly across the bottom of the crust. Combine the beaten eggs with the cream or evaporated milk and green chile and pour this mixture into the crust. Arrange the onion rings and crumbled bacon on top. Cover the edge of the pie crust with a strip of aluminum foil to prevent overbrowning. Bake at 350 degrees. After 25 or 30 minutes, remove the foil from the edge of the pie crust and continue baking for about another 10-15 minutes. Check for doneness by inserting a knife in the center of the pie. When it comes out clean, the pie is done.

Tacos

Serves 6

INGREDIENTS:

1 dozen corn tortillas

1 cup cooking oil

1 tablespoon olive oil

1 pound lean ground beef

1 cup diced green chile

2 cups fresh, frozen, or canned corn

2 small cloves fresh garlic, minced

1 teaspoon salt

$1/2$ cup white or yellow onion, chopped medium to fine

$1/2$ pound longhorn cheese

1 small head of iceberg lettuce, shredded, washed, and drained

4 small fresh tomatoes, diced

DIRECTIONS:

Fry the corn tortillas in hot oil to preferred doneness. Some people prefer soft tacos, but we usually like them delicately crisp. Fold the tortillas in half to form shells. I prefer to use two dinner forks to handle the tortillas rather than tongs or long-handled cooking forks. The inexperienced cook might find a taco-shell form handy; they're sold in specialty shops almost everywhere.

Fry the ground beef, cook well but be sure not to overcook. Add the corn, green chile, onion, and garlic. Mix well and cook for a few minutes more. Divide the filling evenly to spoon into the taco shells. Place filled tacos on a serving dish and top with lettuce, tomatoes, and cheese. We usually serve our tacos with beans and rice.

Navajo Tacos with Fry Bread

Serves 6

Indian Fry Bread

INGREDIENTS:

2 cups flour

1/2 teaspoon salt

2 1/2 teaspoons baking powder

2 tablespoons shortening

3/4 cup warm water

oil for frying

DIRECTIONS:

Combine the dry ingredients and the shortening. Mix well with your fingers.
Blend in the water with a fork. Knead it all until smooth. Divide the dough
into 6 equal balls and roll each ball into an 8-inch circle approximately 1/2-
inch thick, about twice the thickness of a tortilla. Fry the circles in hot oil
until golden brown, turning so both sides are evenly cooked, and drain on
paper towels.

Filling

INGREDIENTS:

1 quart freshly (slightly soupy) cooked beans

1 small head of shredded lettuce

2 chopped tomatoes

1 chopped onion

1/2 pound of grated longhorn cheese

fresh salsa

DIRECTIONS:

Prepare the beans and salsa according to the recipes on pages 69 and 29. Chop the tomatoes and onions and refrigerate. Prepare each plate by placing one piece of fry bread on an oven-safe dish and topping it with 1/2 cup of beans. Keep the dishes warm in the oven as you prepare each one. When they're ready to be served, add the lettuce, tomatoes, onions, and grated cheese. Serve the salsa in a bowl so that it can be added at each person's discretion.

Chicken Tostadas

Makes 12 tostadas

INGREDIENTS:

1 frying chicken to make 4 cups cooked and shredded chicken
4 cloves of garlic
1 teaspoon salt
1 cup grated longhorn cheese
6 green onions, chopped fine
1/2 cup sliced black olives
3 cups shredded lettuce
3 medium tomatoes, chopped small
1 dozen corn tortillas

DIRECTIONS:

Cover the fryer with water in a large pot, add the garlic and salt, and stew until the meat is cooked and tender, about one hour. Be careful not to over-cook. Bone the chicken, shred the meat into bite-sized pieces, and set aside. Fry the corn tortillas flat in hot oil in a large skillet until crisp and then let them drain on paper towels. Place them on a cookie sheet, spoon 2 table-spoons of shredded chicken onto each one, and top with grated cheese.

Just before serving, place them in the oven long enough to warm thoroughly and melt the cheese. Then top each tostada with olives, onions, lettuce, and tomatoes and serve. Guacamole or sour cream is also tasty with them.

Taquitos with Chicken or Beef

Some people call these *flautas*, which means flutes. They are supposed to be quite crisp and are a bit of a trick to handle, so don't be dismayed if it takes a while to learn the technique. They're a good party snack but can make a meal as well, served with beans and rice.

Makes 1 dozen

INGREDIENTS:

1 dozen corn tortillas

1 pound browned lean ground beef or cooked and shredded chicken

1/2 medium onion, chopped fairly fine

vegetable oil for frying

shredded lettuce

chopped tomatoes

DIRECTIONS:

Fry the corn tortillas in hot oil to soften and then drain them on paper towels. Spoon approximately 2 tablespoons of chicken or ground beef and 1 teaspoon of onion onto each tortilla. Roll the filled tortillas into "flutes" and secure with toothpicks. Use a pair of tongs to hold each flute in heated oil just long enough to cook it to a crisp. Drain them on paper towels and top with shredded lettuce and chopped tomato. Serve guacamole and sour cream on the side.

Beef Fajitas

This recipe is not a manito concoction. I remember having generous amounts of sliced meat (usually venison) wrapped in fresh tortillas, which I think we needed to eat up in quantity when we had no more room in the freezer or couldn't salt and dry any more into jerky. No one called the combination "fajitas" then—we just called it *carnitas*. But now fajitas is one of our favorite dishes for family gatherings.

Serves 6-8

INGREDIENTS:

1 pound boneless beef round steak
6-10 medium flour tortillas
1 cup fresh green chile, diced
3/4 cup chopped tomato
2 avocados, peeled and sliced
1 cup Monterey jack cheese, grated
1 cup salsa (any brand)
2 tablespoons vegetable oil

DIRECTIONS:

Cut the round steak into strips as if for a "stir fry" (less than 1/2-inch wide across the grain and about 2 inches long) and fry in oil over medium heat approximately 5 minutes or until well cooked. Add the onions and stir a few seconds longer. Add the chile and continue to cook for a couple more minutes.

Turn off the heat and let the mixture set for a minute or two. Prepare the tortillas by warming slightly on a griddle or in a microwave. Serve the meat on a hot serving plate. Allow guests to serve themselves by placing 2 or 3 tablespoons of the meat in the center of a tortilla, adding sliced tomato, garnishing with avocado, and then folding it into a convenient size and shape. They may want to top it off with sour cream or salsa. Beans and a light salad are good side dishes with fajitas.

Posole

Posole is a traditional winter holiday meal whose essential ingredients are hominy, chile, and pork. Many New Mexican families hold an open-house celebration on Christmas Eve and serve this most traditional of dishes, cooked with a pork roast and thick red chile and served with fresh tortillas or French bread. When we were growing up, friends and relatives dropped by each other's homes to share a little good cheer on the way to and from midnight mass. Christmas Day was usually reserved for the immediate family, with the exception of godparents who brought gifts to their *hijados,* always receiving a gift from the godchild to the *padrinos* in exchange. Posole or menudo was also usually served on New Year's Eve and New Year's Day and, in fact, it still is.

Serves 6-8

INGREDIENTS:

4 fresh pig's feet

4 medium garlic cloves, minced

1 tablespoon salt (or to taste)

2 pounds fresh posole (uncooked hominy), available in most southwestern
supermarkets and meat markets

1 small lean pork roast (3 pounds is usually adequate), cubed

4 red chile pods, sliced lengthwise, with stems and seeds removed

4 cups prepared red chile sauce (as prepared for chile colorado, p. 44)

2 teaspoons oregano

DIRECTIONS:

Rinse the posole several times, cover with water in a stock pot, add 2 teaspoons of salt, and allow it to soak overnight.

When you're ready to begin, drain and rinse the posole and add the pig's feet and garlic. Fill the pot $3/4$ full of water; cover and bring to a boil. Reduce the heat and simmer until the meat is very tender, approximately 6 hours. Place the pot in the refrigerator and when cool, skim the skin and fat from the stock. You may wish to remove the bones also when the stock has cooled, because they can be very small and troublesome.

While the posole and stock are cooking, cover the pork roast with water in a Dutch oven and cook on low heat until just done and very tender, about 2 hours. Cool this meat and its broth in the refrigerator as well and skim the fat from the broth. Cut the roast into small chunks. Then add the skimmed broth, chopped meat, and minced garlic, and 4 chile pods to the posole and pig's feet mixture. Simmer together for $1/2$ hour. Serve in a tureen with a soup ladle with the chile sauce in a separate bowl to be added as desired. Grandma Flora always served posole with fresh rolls or bread. Indian oven bread (bread baked in a traditional Pueblo Indian *horno*) is especially good with it.

Arroz con Pollo (Chicken with Rice)

We often prepare this manito version of "chicken soup" for sick relatives and friends. It's not really a soup at all, but it is very moist. Flora used to make this whenever anyone wasn't feeling well.

Serves 6

INGREDIENTS:

$1/2$ cup vegetable oil

1 frying chicken cut into parts, washed, and dried

2 cups long-grain white rice

1 large white onion, cut into slivers, approx. $1/2$ x 3 in.

1 large bell pepper, cut into slivers, approx. $1/2$ x 3 in.

1 large carrot, cut into similarly sized sticks

1 large fresh garlic clove, pressed or minced

1 heaping tablespoon corn starch

1 tablespoon fresh Mexican oregano (use a little more if dried)

2 cups water

2 teaspoons salt

DIRECTIONS:

Heat the oil to medium high in a large Dutch oven and brown the chicken parts, turning to cook evenly. Add the uncooked rice and brown evenly. Then add the carrots and sauté approximately 2 minutes; add the bell pepper and sauté the mixture for a few minutes more. Add the onions and continue to cook evenly. Finally, blend the garlic into the mixture.

Clear a space in the center of the pan and add the corn starch, blending well with the liquid and oil. When the mixture is smooth, mix the cornstarch, vegetables, and chicken all together. Add salt, cover, and cook on medium low heat for 30 to 40 minutes until the chicken is thoroughly cooked. Then turn off the heat, sprinkle the oregano on top before blending it in gently, and allow to set for 15 minutes before serving.

Fideos

This dish is the ultimate in quick meals, light but satisfying. It isn't seasonal—I remember having it just as often in spring or summer as in the colder months.

Fideos is another one of those dishes that varies from family to family. Some prefer it quite thin and almost soupy; others like it thicker, more like an Italian spaghetti dish. Some people like a heavy tomato flavor; and others like more of a broth, with vegetables such as celery and fresh tomatoes chopped small. This recipe is Grandma Flora's version.

Serves 6 or more

INGREDIENTS:

1 12-ounce package of fideos (thin nested vermicelli)

1/2 cup vegetable oil

1 16-ounce can tomato sauce

2 cups water

1 small onion, diced

1 teaspoon salt

1/2 pound grated longhorn cheese

1/2-1 pound ground beef or ground turkey (optional)

DIRECTIONS:

Heat oil to medium hot in a large Dutch oven or skillet. While the oil is heating, break up the nested noodles into smaller chunks in a large mixing bowl. Have your tomato sauce open and ready to use.

When the oil is medium hot, sauté the onions and then move them to the side of the pot. Carefully place the broken noodles into the oil and brown evenly. NOTE: You must stir the noodles constantly, as they burn easily! Blend the onions into the cooked noodles and quickly add the can of tomato sauce. Add the 2 cups of water and the salt. Mix the noodles and sauce well. Turn the heat down to simmer and cook for no more than 15 minutes. Pour into a serving bowl, sprinkle grated cheese on top, and serve immediately.

To make this a more substantial dish, add 1/2 to 1 pound of browned ground beef. Brown the ground beef (or ground turkey) separately and gently add it to the fideos before adding the cheese. Fideos go well with a salad and fresh French bread or homemade tortillas.

Huevos Rancheros with Papas Fritas

Many of the standard restaurant and modern-day names for New Mexican food were absent from our early-day vocabulary. For example, I never heard of a burrito; we just rolled whatever was tasty and available into our version of daily bread, the tortilla. We did use the term *"huevos rancheros,"* however. It was the kind of big, hearty breakfast that is still served on farms and ranches all over New Mexico to get ready for a hard day's work.

INGREDIENTS:
2 or 3 farm-fresh eggs per person
fresh corn tortillas
freshly prepared green or red chile sauce or a good salsa
grated asadero or longhorn cheese

DIRECTIONS:
Fry and drain the corn tortillas. Place them in an oven-safe dish, cover with paper towels and aluminum foil, and put in a warm oven. Fry or scramble each serving of eggs to desired doneness. Top with the chile and cheese of each guest's choice. Serve with warm tortillas, frijoles, and *papas fritas.* Grandma Flora preferred small red potatoes thinly sliced with the skins on and pan fried until crispy.

Las Nuevas Tamaleras

A couple of years ago I took my fifth-grade class to see a play called *Las Nuevas Tamaleras,* performed by a theater group here in Albuquerque. The story featured a trio of modern young Chicana career women who

were beginning to feel the loss of their culture. They decided to recapture the sweet memories of their childhood by making tamales for the Christmas holiday.

The problem is that even their combined memory of tamale making isn't enough to do the job right. Enter two ghost abuelas who are bored with their heavenly existence and are "dying" to have a little old-fashioned fun. The elder grandma ghost, Doña Somebody, knows the oldest *tradiciones,* the unadulterated and unacculturated way to make tamales. The other grandma ghost is from a later time and admits that she purchased her *masa preparada* from the Landmark Grocery store. Together they "teach" las nuevas tamaleras how to make a community by cooperation and the expectation of excellence.

The play humorously proves the point that New Mexicans take their tamales very seriously. One of the quickest ways to get into a heated discussion is to say to another New Mexican that your mother, sister, abuela, or *tía* makes the best tamales. You are quickly met with a barrage of challenges to your outrageous claim. I don't know why there are no formal tamale cookoffs, but if there were, I would enter this recipe. It's a reduced-fat version that is still muy sabroso.

Tamale parties have become rather trendy. Lots of people in the Southwest have them now and send each guest home with a Christmas gift of a dozen gaily wrapped tamales, for eating right away or freezing. (They're a good way to sample other people's recipes!) Grandma Flora never gave an "official" tamale party, but every time she made tamales it was like a party, with the same spirit of community and fun.

I have written this recipe exactly the way I make my own tamales, as originally modified into this low-fat version by my niece Natalie Saucedo.

I find that people quickly develop specific ideas about what "the perfect tamale" should be, so it may take some modifications to achieve the perfect tamale for you. Be patient and don't expect miracles the first time you try. But any tamales are good tamales, so you will surely enjoy your first effort however it turns out. This recipe takes practice, like making good tortillas.

Read the directions through carefully, assemble all necessary equipment and ingredients, and remember: making tamales requires several hours, depending on how many dozens of tamales you make and the number of other tamaleras or tamaleros available to help you get the job done.

First you must determine how many tamales you want to make. It's a lot of work, so people usually opt to make several dozen at a time. I recently gave a baby shower for my daughter-in-law and made six dozen tamales because I expected about thirty people. Needless to say, the tamales were the first item to disappear, leaving my guests disappointed that they were all gone so quickly.

The following recipe will provide approximately five to six dozen 6-ounce tamales.

Tamales *(low-fat pero todavía sabrosos)*

INGREDIENTS:
Filling:
1 frying chicken
1 small lean pork roast (approximately 3 pounds)
10 large cloves of garlic
12-ounce bag or 40 medium red chile pods
cooking broth (see below)

Masa:

4.4-pound bag of masa harina (cornmeal flour)

2 teaspoons baking powder

cooking broth (see below)

2 cups red chile sauce

salt to taste

Hojas:

2 6-ounce packages of corn husks

PREPARATIONS:

The day before your "tamale party," buy a small bone-in pork roast (approximately 3 pounds of meat is needed), one plump roasting chicken (approximately 2 pounds of meat is needed), 4-5 pounds of masa harina, approximately 12 to 16 ounces of the freshest possible red chile pods, at least 10 cloves of fresh garlic, fresh oregano, and 2 packages of corn husks *(hojas).* One package is sometimes enough for 5 or 6 dozen tamales but not always, and too many is certainly more convenient than not enough.

That night (the night before you make the tamales), cook the pork roast and the chicken together. Place the meat in a large stock pot and cover with water. Add 6 cloves of fresh garlic, salt gently, and cook on medium low heat for 1 1/2 hours. Be careful to turn the meat every half hour or so to cook it evenly and keep it moist. The meat should be tender but not overcooked, as it will be cooked again later when the tamales are steamed.

Allow the meat to cool for handling. Drain off the broth and allow it to cool in the refrigerator. Remove and discard the chicken skin, fat, and bone. Break the chicken meat into small bite-sized chunks, but do not shred. Do the same with the pork roast. Combine the meats in a large rectangular cake pan, cover, and refrigerate overnight.

DIRECTIONS:

Before you actually begin filling the tamales, be sure to analyze your cooking area for the best way to set up your assembly line for spreading the masa and chile on the hoja. You will need space for setting out the hojas (corn husks), soaked and washed and ready to dry with a supply of clean towels, along with the pans of chile and masa and a tray for the finished tamales. A long counter, bar, or table will work. You also have to arrange the space for whatever help you have. Spreading is sort of a messy job and requires frequent hand washing and wiping. The chile spatters a little, too, so you may want to cover things that might get stained. I use old bath towels.

The day after buying and preparing the meats, begin by soaking the hojas (corn husks) in very hot water in a sink or large pan. Then rinse and keep them in a pan until ready to use.

Next, heat the chicken broth in a large pot. Clean the chile pods of their stems and seeds, rinse, and then soak them in the very hot (but not boiling) broth, not quite covering the chile pods. The chile pods will need to be stirred to soften evenly. Allow the pods to sit until all are very soft, usually a few hours.

Blend the completely softened chile pods in a blender with 4 cloves of garlic and enough of the soaking broth to make approximately 2 quarts of a thick gravy-like consistency. Strain the chile through a food mill to remove the waxy skin (see the chile colorado recipe on p. 44). Reserve 2 cups of the prepared chile sauce for the masa. Add the remaining chile to the combined meat chunks that you prepared the day before. Refrigerate the chile and meat mixture for easier spreadability.

Mix 2 teaspoons of baking powder thoroughly into the masa harina. Add 2 cups of the prepared chile and then add enough warm broth until the dough is approximately the consistency of soft cookie dough. Salt it lightly (saltiness will strengthen with cooking) and cover to keep moist.

Place the containers of hojas, masa, and the chile-meat mixture ready to spread and roll into tamales in your already prepared work area. (PLEASE

NOTE: If I'm making tamales alone or with only one helper, I take only the amounts of masa and chile out of the refrigerator that can be spread in an hour or so, to keep the ingredients fresh.) I often direct one person to dry off the moist hoja with towels and then hand that hoja to another worker who will spread the inside center of an approximately 8-inch square hoja (or layer of two hojas) with masa approximately 1/8 to 1/4 of an inch thick. The second person carefully hands the masa-covered hoja to another spreader who puts a generous tablespoon of meat and chile in the center of each. Then the hoja is folded up at the bottom and rolled to produce a 2x6-inch, rolled-up tamale. Some folks tie each end with a long sliver of corn husk or string, but that is a matter of choice—and a lot of extra work.

A large tamale pot will hold 5 or 6 dozen. (Numerous stores carry this standard tamale pot with steamer.) Fill the steamer with the required amount of water (to a level just below the steamer basket because you don't want the tamales standing in the water) and then stand the tamales on end against each other inside the steamer basket. Start by placing the first tamales against the inside of the pot, leaning one against the other, spiral fashion into the center of the pot. All the tamales should be leaning away from the center. Leave a space in the center in order to check the water level. Place the pot on a large burner and turn to medium low heat. Remember to check the water level periodically and add water as necessary. Cook for approximately 90 minutes after the water has begun to steam.

Of course, you must start checking after about 75 minutes to see if the tamales are done. "Testers" are carefully selected and very privileged people who discern the degree of doneness and the degree of success of your tamales. We always toast the success of a batch with our favorite beverages while we wait.

No winter holiday in New Mexico is complete without tamales. They should be served with a pot of freshly made beans. We often serve them covered with red chile and serve Spanish rice as well as the beans. A tossed salad is refreshing to round out the meal. I hope you will enjoy our family's reduced-fat version.

Chapter 5

La Estufa Vieja

SIDE DISHES AND SOUPS

Dolores (Sister Anthony) with brothers
Antonio to the left and Fernando to the right

Grandma Flora didn't leave us many recipes for side dishes, particularly vegetable dishes. We lived in a small town, not a rural area, and Grandma didn't have a garden, so that may be why we didn't have many fresh vegetables. But I also remember my father referring to salads as "rabbit food," so apparently there was some disdain for vegetables in general. But any disdain for vegetables of course did not include beans.

Frijoles

Beans were the most fundamental part of manito cuisine and were welcomed at almost every meal—breakfast, lunch, and dinner—along with the other staples, tortillas and chile. There always seemed to be a pot of beans either cooking or being rewarmed on everyone's wood cookstove. Manita women were slow to convert to gas and electric stoves because of the comfort most enjoyed in using those old stoves.

Even within my own generation, it was pretty common to know how to use *una estufa vieja.* They were an ordinary part of our lives. We were all able to chop wood and pick the right type of coal to build a fire that was hot enough, but not too hot. We knew how to judge the correct time and therefore the correct temperature at which to prepare various foods. Beans were slow cooked all day long at the back of the stove. No one had an electric crockpot back then.

Stoves were the center of the kitchen: they cooked our beans and chile and baked our empanadas and roasted the piñon nuts just right. Electric or gas stoves could never do the job as well. In addition to cooking foods and keeping them warm at just the right temperature, la estufa vieja kept the

house warm as well. Many manita women still use the old stovetop lids, called *comales* (or *el comal*), on top of a gas or electric burner just to make tortillas, because as far as they are concerned, nothing else will do.

Grandma Flora always bought hundred-pound sacks of pinto beans, as did most of the families we knew. Of course, most people don't buy beans in such quantity anymore, but I should point out that the beans should be as fresh as possible. Here again, ask your produce vendors which beans are the most fresh and flavorful. Very new beans will render a pinkish and tender flavor. Older beans will cook up to a deep brown and a more hearty flavor. But when beans cook up to a very dark brown or even a sort of grayish tone, they are too old.

There was definitely a technique to cooking beans properly, and that included cooking the beans according to the food they accompanied. For example, when beans were to be served with a red or green chile with a thicker gravy-like texture, we would prepare them to a medium consistency to hold the weight of the chile. If the beans were very soupy, they were served as that—a soup accompanied by *una salsa muy picante* and, of course, a few fresh tortillas or hard rolls. *¡Manita comida original!*

Manitas usually rewarmed rather than refried beans. If the beans needed thickening, they would be cooked down and perhaps thickened slightly with a little flour.

Sopa de Frijoles (Bean Soup)

Makes 2 quarts
INGREDIENTS:
1 pound fresh pinto beans

1 large ham bone or 2 ham hocks
1 quart water
2 large cloves garlic
salt to taste

DIRECTIONS:

Pick out small pebbles and shriveled or broken beans from your supply and then rinse the beans thoroughly in cold water; drain in a colander. Cover beans with water in a large Dutch oven, heat, and allow to boil for ten minutes. Drain and rinse the beans in hot water and then transfer the beans to a crock pot. (You can also use a pressure cooker.) Add the garlic, salt, and ham bones and simmer for several hours (3 or 4), adding boiling or very hot water when required to keep beans constantly covered. If you don't have a crock pot, you have to stay vigilant to maintain your stove burner at just the right simmer.

Keep the beans covered and cooking for a total of 6 to 8 hours. Before serving, salt them to slightly less than you might like just to be sure. It seems to be so easy to oversalt beans.

Refritos

This recipe goes well with tacos, tostadas, taquitos, burritos, and huevos rancheros.

Serves 6

INGREDIENTS:

4 cups cooked beans
1 tablespoon oil
onion
grated cheese
milk can be added for flavor

DIRECTIONS:

Cover a large skillet with approximately 1 tablespoon of oil per 4 cups of beans. How you proceed from this point depends on how you prefer your beans. You heat the oil in the skillet and add the beans and other ingredients as desired. If you like beans rather dry and even somewhat crispy, be sure they are drained of as much liquid as possible and let them sizzle to desired doneness. If you want a more moist variation, add a little broth or milk to the desired consistency and heat through. If you have a taste for cheese, sprinkle grated cheese over the heated beans and then blend slightly, but not too much.

Sopas

Menudo

Menudo was less popular in our house than posole, but as we got older we developed more of a taste for it. It is the traditional dish served on New Year's Eve and is said to bring good luck for the year ahead.

Serves 12

INGREDIENTS:

2 pounds menudo (tripe) cut into 2-inch squares
2 pounds of nixtamal (uncooked hominy)
4 pig's feet
3 cloves of garlic, chopped
salt to taste
1 medium onion, chopped fine
1 lemon to cut into wedges
Mexican oregano
crushed chile pequín
salt to taste

DIRECTIONS:

Soak and wash the tripe thoroughly and cut into squares. Wash the uncooked hominy thoroughly to remove any trace of lime. Combine the tripe, hominy, pig's feet, and garlic in a stockpot and cook on medium low heat for about 5 hours until the hominy has popped and the tripe is cooked. Then salt the broth slightly less than you will want, since it strengthens as it continues to cook for approximately another 1/2 hour. Meanwhile, chop the onions and slice a lemon into half wedges. Serve the onion, lemon, dried oregano, and crushed chile pequín separately for your guests to add to their bowls of hot menudo as they wish. Some people also serve menudo with about a half cup of freshly made chile colorado, either with or without pork.

Sopa de Papas

As winter set in, we could count on having potato soup again. When the cold winds began to blow across the mesas and the snow began to fall, this old-fashioned sopa was sure to keep us warm and comforted. Grandma used red potatoes, her usual choice for almost all potato dishes. Serve *sopa de papas* with fresh hot rolls or manito cornbread.

Serves 8

INGREDIENTS:

8 medium potatoes
4 carrots
4 celery stalks
1 quart of water
3 cups milk, scalded
4 egg yolks
2 small white onions
butter
salt to taste
fresh ground pepper

DIRECTIONS:

Peel and dice the potatoes, carrots, and celery and place them in a large saucepan or stockpot. Cover with 1 quart of water and bring to a boil. Lower the heat to a simmer and cook the vegetables until very soft. Strain the vegetables and reserve the stock. Mash the potatoes and carrots together until smooth and return them to the stock. Add the scalded milk and beat in the egg yolks. Salt to taste. Slice the onion into crescents and sauté in butter until lightly browned. Then add the onion to the soup and heat through. Serve each bowl topped with a pad of butter and a dash of freshly ground black pepper.

Sopa de Albóndigas (Meatball Soup)

This soup is a flavorful testimony to the Spanish lineage of los nuevos mexicanos. Unlike many other dishes in manito cuisine, there is not a lot of variation in its preparation, except that some families don't use oregano or add green chile.

Serves 6

Sopa

INGREDIENTS:

2 tablespoons shortening

1 medium red onion, chopped

4 celery stalks, chopped fine

3 long green chiles, chopped

1 large can stewed tomatoes

2 teaspoons fresh cilantro, chopped fine

1 teaspoon dried Mexican oregano

1 teaspoon salt

1 quart water

Albóndigas:

1 pound ground round

1 cup white rice, cooked and well rinsed

1 egg

1/2 cup white onion, chopped fine

1 teaspoon dried Mexican oregano

Directions:

Sauté the red onion in the melted shortening in a Dutch oven. Add all the other sopa ingredients with the water and bring to a boil. Lower the heat, cover, and simmer for 15 minutes.

Meanwhile combine all meatball ingredients and form them into balls about the size of walnuts. Increase the heat of the broth to a second boil and drop the meatballs gently into the pot. After all the meatballs are in the broth, lower the heat to a simmer and cook for approximately another 30 minutes.

Sopa de albóndigas is perfect with fresh hard rolls.

Side Dishes

Quelites con Frijoles

Quelites are a wild type of leafy greens, very similar to spinach. Their common English name is lamb's quarters or purslane. Another variety is the amaranth plant (pigweed). Both grow wild all over the Southwest, usually in cleared areas where there's moisture. Grandma Flora gathered quelites from the banks of ditches and canals near our house. Some people cultivate them, but I don't believe that Grandma ever did because they were so plentiful wild. Apparently, when she found a large batch of this "Spanish spinach," she would dry it in the sun and store it in little cloth bags, made from flour sacks, on hooks in her old *cuartito* (little outside shed).

Quelites and beans was a favorite Lenten dish. A big cast iron skillet of this *cuaresmale* often bubbled on the cookstove in the early spring, when northern New Mexico is often still cold and blustery. Sometimes Grandma served quelites alongside scrambled eggs, smothered in a salsa picante.

You can substitute spinach, since quelites are not always available.

Makes 6 cups

INGREDIENTS:

2 cups cooked and drained quelites or spinach

1 pound bacon

2 tablespoons bacon drippings

1/2 cup onion, cut into thin crescents

1 tablespoon crushed chile pequín

4 cups cooked pinto beans

DIRECTIONS:

Fry the bacon until crispy, drain it, and set aside. Reserve approximately 2 tablespoons of the drippings. Sauté the onion in the bacon drippings and, in succession, add spinach or quelites, chile, and beans and blend together. Sprinkle the top with the cooled and crumbled bacon, heat through, and serve.

Tortas de Huevos

This *torta* concoction is a Lenten dish, another of the many delicious cuaresmales. Grandma was meticulous about serving meat-free meals on any fasting day, and this was one of them. I don't remember eating it at any other time. The secret to good tortas is to prepare a moderately thick red chile sauce and to cook the tortas to a firm—but not rubbery—doneness before dropping them into the chile sauce to serve.

Serves 8

INGREDIENTS:

cooking oil

6 fresh eggs

1 tablespoon flour

1 teaspoon baking powder

1 teaspoon salt

1 quart cooked red chile (as in chile colorado, p. 44)

DIRECTIONS:

Break and separate the whites and yolks of the eggs. Beat the whites until fluffy and then fold in the flour, baking powder, salt, and yolks. Drop dollops of the egg mixture into a skillet of very hot oil with a cooking spoon and cook until the egg is fully cooked but not rubbery. Remove each one separately with a slotted spoon and drain on paper towels. When all the egg mixture is

cooked in this fashion (called tortas), place them in a skillet of hot red chile sauce to coat them and then serve immediately in shallow bowls, such as you might use for soup. I've seen some people add small dried shrimp to the torta mix, but Grandma Flora never used shrimp, just thick and hot red chile.

Spanish Rice

Serves 8

INGREDIENTS:

1 tablespoon olive oil

1 1/2 cups uncooked long-grain white rice

1 small white onion, chopped fine

2 medium cloves garlic, minced

1 8-ounce can of tomato sauce

3 cups water

2 cups tomatoes, diced

1 teaspoon cumin

1 teaspoon salt

1 teaspoon saffron

DIRECTIONS:

Heat the oil in a large frying pan on medium heat. Brown the rice, stirring constantly, for about 3 or 4 minutes. Add the onion and garlic and sauté with the rice; then add the tomato sauce and water and bring to a boil. Quickly lower the heat to a simmer, add the fresh tomatoes, salt, and cumin and cook for 20 minutes, stirring occasionally. Remove it from the heat, sprinkle the saffron on top, and let it stand (covered) for 15 minutes before serving.

Calabacitas

Calabacitas is an easy and delicious summer meal when fresh zucchini and corn are plentiful. Toruma, a lightly striped green squash about the size of a small cantalope, is a good choice if no small, fresh zucchini are available. Or you might combine two kinds of squash, such as the yellow crookneck squash and zucchini. Grandma Flora often used squash which she had dried on the portal in strips and then kept in the cool pantry. She would reconstitute the strips in water before sautéing them.

You can substitute a good creamier cheese instead of the longhorn if you prefer. Monterey Jack or asadero are good choices.

Serves 6

INGREDIENTS:

2 tablespoons cooking oil
4 small to medium zucchini or crookneck squash,
    cubed (or other tender squash)
1 medium onion, diced
2 cloves garlic, minced
1 cup chopped, roasted, peeled green chile
1 large tomato, diced
2 cups fresh or frozen corn kernels
1 cup longhorn cheese, grated
salt to taste

DIRECTIONS:

Heat the oil in a large heavy skillet. Sauté the zucchini (and any other squash), onion, garlic, chile, and tomato for just a few minutes. Stir in the corn and cook for 15 minutes uncovered. Add the cheese and continue to cook the mixture just until the cheese melts. Serve immediately. Calabacitas go well with any meat and are hearty enough to be served alone with fresh tortillas or rolls.

Avocado and Tomato Salad

Serves 6

INGREDIENTS:

2 large avocados

2 large tomatoes

1/2 a white onion

3 fresh jalapeños

1 teaspoon salt

1 teaspoon garlic salt

DIRECTIONS:

Dice the avocados, tomatoes, and onion small. Then mince the jalapeño chile and blend all the ingredients together in a medium salad bowl. Mix in the seasoning. Serve with steak or any meat dish. It also makes a good dip, served with corn chips.

Chapter 6

Oraciones y Pan

PRAYERS AND BREADS

Cousin Lorraine at
Round Rock Trading Post

When we were children, it was always a special treat for us to stay overnight with Grandma. We all loved the special attention she gave us and the little treats she always had, like biscochitos.

She would prepare each of us for bed with a thorough scrubbing in her *bandejita,* an enamel wash pan that each of us girls had to fill, in turn, with hot soapy water and then empty. She brushed our hair and dressed us in our Uncle Román's soft, white, cotton T-shirts. She always wore a long, cotton flannel nightgown, even in summer. I loved to watch her unpin her salt-and-pepper hair from its bun. She would let one of us brush her hair and braid it into a long, thick braid down her back. Then we would kneel by the side of the bed as she said a prayer with us before she tucked all of us into her big iron bed.

Grandma then knelt alone at her altar of the Blessed Mother, praying her rosary before she got into bed. I always tried to stay awake and say her prayers with her. I usually fell asleep hearing "Hail Mary, full of grace, the Lord is with thee. Blessed art thou amongst women...." When we woke the next morning, we always saw her there before her altar again, still wearing her flannel nightgown with her braid down her back and the black wooden rosary in her hands. When I was very small, I wondered if she had knelt there all night long. She always seemed so serene, kneeling in prayer. I remember that I could not understand how she knelt so long in seeming comfort, when kneeling for the briefest of prayers was such a torture for me.

Grandma observed all the religious holidays, not with dreary solemnity but with a dignified expression of joy. Aunt Lolie remembers that Grandma worked very hard all week long, but that she was meticulous about saving the Sabbath day for rest and prayer. The only time anyone ever heard Grandma speak disapprovingly to my father was to chide him mildly for

not going to church on Sunday or for working on one of his many building projects on Sunday. Work was simply not allowed on Sunday; other days were a different story.

Yet she didn't have that feeling of frenzy that is so prevalent today in people who accomplish so much, who work so much. I know that she enjoyed what she did; and although she did seem fatigued sometimes, especially as she grew older, she was always serene.

We always knew that a strong work ethic was not the exclusive domain of the Puritans. Our little Grandma worked constantly, but she organized her chores and accomplished them with a sense of pride, often even managing to make them fun. She kept an immaculately clean house, but we children were still allowed to play—dressing up in her clothes, moving furniture to play house and camp and to put on plays. She didn't fuss over us, like so many scrupulously clean housekeepers; we just helped her put everything away when we were finished. Everything she did—from thoroughly boiling and washing the homemade *colchones de lana* (wool mattresses) in homemade lye soap and then drying the soft wool in the sun every spring, to washing walls and polishing woodwork and hardwood floors in her living room—was done in a matter-of-fact way, without any hint of complaint.

Her living room was a sanctuary of thick adobe walls and heavy mahogany woodwork. She kept a couple of overstuffed velvety chairs with lion-paw feet covered with sheets in preparation for guests or a family evening around the console radio, the floor model kind. A big Two Gray Hills Navajo rug covered much of the polished floor, and the windows were covered with heavy velvet drapes in a deep wine color. There was a heavy, brown woodstove in the corner. A huge Webster's dictionary, dated

1932, lay on a carved side table, waiting for someone to read its precious contents. I still have that book, tattered from years of use.

I remember listening intently to her soft singsong voice as she spoke to us in that room, teaching us what we needed to learn. Unlike so many adults, she talked with us children and actually listened to what we had to say. But she was always working. She would automatically reach for a needle and thread at the sight of a loose button on a dress or shirt. It seemed her small, fair-skinned, freckled hands never stopped. I have a picture etched in my memory of me and my family in that living room, reading and listening to the old radio with Grandma Flora knitting, crocheting, sewing, and going periodically into the kitchen to tend some dish she was preparing.

When she wasn't there with us, Grandma Flora was with Uncle Román. He had come back from the war in Germany (World War II) with a serious injury from the recoil of heavy artillery and had never recovered. He lived with Grandma until he died in 1953. They always spoke to each other in Spanish and were very close. When he died, I expected her to be very sad. She missed him terribly, but she was secure in her firm belief that he was with God. She comforted me by saying, *"No lloras, mijita,* your Tío Román is resting with God now."

As I never saw her show great grief, I also never saw Grandma Flora show anger. Dad once said that the only way to tell if his mamá was angry was by the pink spots that appeared on her forehead. After that, I would look for the telltale pink spots, but I never saw them.

My father claimed that she hadn't always been so controlled. He chuckled when recounting how she sailed more than one cooking pan in his direction after he had pulled some childhood prank. We couldn't imagine

that! She literally practiced her faith enough that she could control her emotions. As devoted as she was to her God, however, she never preached; she taught by example. And somehow she always managed to look dignified—even when she would rush to daily mass with flour from her latest batch of tortillas clinging to her cheek and her black church hat, with a small faded silk cabbage rose stuck in the hatband, perched slightly askew on her head.

Tortillas

Tortillas were the quintessential comfort food for all of us Romero kids—and there is no doubt that Grandma Flora's were the very best. Rolling tortillas is a tricky process and requires a little practice, so it was quite an accomplishment when a little girl in my family learned how to roll tortillas expertly. The *creencia* goes something like this, *"Cuando una señorita está hechando tortillas y salen chamuscadas, cuando se case, va a hacer mala nuera."* (If a young lady is making tortillas and they burn, she will be a bad daughter-in-law when she marries.)

My sister Marsha is a tortilla expert. She usually rolls tortillas thinner than the fat, fluffy ones that our Grandma Flora made, however, because she's adopted the style used by her husband's family. Different families prefer different styles. I didn't learn until I was an adult and still am not an expert, but the flavor of a fresh tortilla is worth the effort.

Tortillas require a special rolling pin that is smaller than a pastry rolling pin and has no handles. They are available at specialty stores or can be made by cutting a 1-inch hardwood dowel into a piece 6 inches long and sanding it smooth.

This recipe makes about 5 or 6 large tortillas or 12 small ones. I usually double the recipe for the soft fluffy-style tortilla that Grandma Flora made. The old *dicho, La práctica hace una maestra,* certainly applies here.

INGREDIENTS:

4 cups unbleached flour

3 tablespoons shortening (Grandma always used lard, but we've found that the flavor is not changed much by substituting a low-cholesterol shortening.)

1½ teaspoons baking powder

1 teaspoon salt

1 to 1½ cups warm water

DIRECTIONS:

Combine dry ingredients in a large bowl, add the shortening, and blend very thoroughly with a pastry blender, knives, or your fingertips. Add water in small increments and knead the dough until it is smooth and pliable. If the dough is not well blended, the tortillas will be brittle instead of pliable, but if they are blended too much they may be a little tough.

Form small balls of equal size, about the size of walnuts. Then cover with a damp towel and let them set for 10 or 15 minutes.

Meanwhile, heat your griddle to medium high or until a drop of water sizzles away instantly.

ROLLING:

This is the part that takes some practice. First dust the rolling pin and the surface area (as close to the griddle as possible) with a light even layer of flour. Put the *bolita* (little ball of tortilla dough) in the middle of the floured area and flatten it into as round a shape as possible by rolling and then turning the rolled disk over several times to keep an even thickness as well as symmetrically round. I still cannot roll tortillas as I saw it done with nearly blinding

speed by my mother, Benina Bustamante Romero, and our Grandma Flora, but I can roll them into even rounds.

After your tortilla is rolled, lift it very carefully with your fingertips and set it on the dry medium-hot griddle. Then you must watch closely until little bubbles form on the tops of each tortilla. By carefully lifting the edge slightly, you'll be able to see if the bottom bubbles have turned a light brown. If so, then turn it over carefully and quickly with your fingertips to cook evenly on both sides. Place the cooked tortillas on a towel beside your rolling area to let them cool slightly before stacking, otherwise they will stick together. Store them inside a towel in a closed container until used.

Of course, tortillas are great right off the griddle smeared with butter, so expect them to be stolen very quickly if left unguarded. You'll find that you can double, triple, and even quadruple this recipe with no loss of quality, once you have learned to mix and handle the dough.

Sopaipillas

These are one of our special occasion foods. When anyone gets a *grano* (a craving for a very specific thing) for sopaipillas, it must be satisfied quickly, we all agree.

Yields about a dozen

INGREDIENTS:

4 cups unbleached flour

1 egg

2 teaspoons baking powder

1 teaspoon salt

4 tablespoons shortening or lard

1 to 1^1/$_2$ cups cold water

oil for frying

DIRECTIONS:

Combine the dry ingredients. Blend in the shortening or lard as thoroughly as when making tortillas. Add liquid along with the egg into the dry ingredients and mix until the dough is smooth. Cover and let it rest for 15 minutes.

Heat 2 inches of oil in a large skillet, usually at about medium high. On a floured board, roll the dough into 6-inch rounds, 1/8 inch thick. Cut them in half with a sharp knife and pierce them slightly in the center with a fork tine or knife point. Then place them very carefully in the hot oil. Watch carefully and turn once as the sopaipillas puff up and turn a golden brown. Drain them on paper towels and serve hot with butter and honey.

Manito Cornbread

The cornbread that all of my family seems to make is our own variation of the plain version. We seem to be compelled to add chile to everything! Medium-hot green chile added to a batter moistened by evaporated milk or buttermilk, along with longhorn cheese and onions, is perfect with a pot of chile verde caldo or fresh sopa de frijoles, good and soupy.

Fills an 8-inch square baking pan

INGREDIENTS:

1 1/2 cups corn meal

1/2 cup all purpose flour

1 tablespoon baking powder

1 teaspoon salt

1/4 cup white onion, chopped

1/2 cup chopped green chile (moderately hot)

1/2 cup grated longhorn cheese

1 cup buttermilk (evaporated milk may be substituted)

1 can creamed corn

2 eggs

$1/2$ cup corn oil

DIRECTIONS:

Preheat oven to 400 degrees. Thoroughly grease an 8-inch square baking dish. Chop the onion and chile and grate the cheese. Combine the corn meal, flour, baking powder, and salt in a medium-sized mixing bowl. Mix well. Add the onion, green chile, grated cheese, canned corn, and milk to the dry mixture. Combine the eggs and oil in a separate bowl until blended and then add to the corn batter. Stir well until it's all evenly blended but not overmixed. Pour into the greased baking dish and bake at 400 degrees for 30 minutes for a moist bread that goes well with barbecued ribs, chicken, or eggs. Bake for 40 minutes for a crisper bread that goes well with soups, soupy pinto beans, or chile verde caldo.

Pan Poco Dulce (Bread)

Fresh bread was one of the foods I loved to watch our grandmother prepare, not only because of the fragrance and the anticipation of flavor but also because of the care it involved. Whenever I make bread or even catch the fragrance of fresh bread in progress, I can close my eyes and see my tiny little grandmother, elbow-deep in dough with flour dusted across her apron, her hair slipping out of its bun, and biting the tip of her tongue and wrinkling her forehead exactly like my father did when concentrating.

Grandma Flora usually made tortillas, but occasionally she would make a hearty, delicious roll as a special treat. She would start them early in the

morning, mixing the dough and then allowing it to rise in a big flowered enamel pan on the stove. We would wake up to the fragrance of the rising bread. Invariably, Grandma would make cinnamon rolls with some of the dough and serve us cinnamon rolls with our morning café.

Makes approximately 12 rolls

INGREDIENTS:

2 packages dry yeast

1/2 cup warm water

1 cup butter

3/4 cup sugar

2 cups milk

6 cups all-purpose flour

2 well-beaten eggs

1 teaspoon salt (optional)

melted butter

DIRECTIONS:

Dissolve the yeast and a pinch of sugar in the warm water. Combine the butter, the rest of the sugar, milk, and salt in a saucepan. Heat just until the butter melts and then cool it to lukewarm.

In a large mixing bowl combine the mixture with 2 cups of the flour and blend well. Blend in the dissolved yeast and the beaten eggs. Gradually add the rest of the flour, about 1/2 cup at a time, until the dough begins to pull away from the sides of the bowl. Turn the dough out onto a lightly floured surface and knead it until smooth and elastic, approximately ten minutes. Put it in a greased bowl in a warm place and let it rise to double in size, approximately 11/2 hours. Be sure that the bowl is in a draft-free spot. Then gently punch the dough down and knead it again. Cover it with a dish towel or plastic and let it rest for 10-15 minutes.

While the dough is resting, preheat the oven to 350 degrees. Then knead the dough one more time and shape it into baseball-sized, elongated rolls. Place the rolls on greased baking sheets and brush the tops with melted butter. Let them rise until doubled in size again and then bake for 25 minutes or until golden brown.

CINNAMON ROLL VARIATION:

For 2 dozen cinnamon rolls, simply roll out half of the dough at a time into a 12x12-inch square. Brush the dough with melted butter and sprinkle liberally with cinnamon and sugar. Add raisins and chopped nuts if you like. Roll up the dough along the side, jelly-roll fashion. With a sharp knife, cut the roll into 1-inch segments and place them on a greased baking sheet. Let them rise until they have doubled in size. Bake in an oven pre-heated to 350 degrees for about 25 minutes, until golden brown.

Chapter 7
Sopa Is Not A Soup

MANITA DESSERTS

Lina Rubí Hubbell (Mrs. John Lorenzo Hubbell),
Melitón's aunt, probably in the 1880s

(COURTESY OF THE ARIZONA HISTORICAL SOCIETY, #6693)

There are not many desserts unique to the Southwest, but the ones that we do commonly enjoy are wonderful. Everyone seems to have a favorite that ties in somehow with special events in childhood. *Natillas* is a huge favorite because it is light and delicate and yet so satisfying. *Sopa* to a New Mexican is not a soup but a bread pudding. Grandma Flora's version is our sister Lorease's favorite and was often served during Lent. *Arroz dulce,* or rice pudding, prepared the manita way is incomparable.

Grandma Flora also made pies, but the crust was more like tortilla dough than the flaky crust most people prefer. Another common dessert she served was strawberry Jell-O with sliced bananas. Aunt Dolores recalls that Grandma prepared Jell-O almost every Sunday during the winter by setting the Jell-O on top of the frozen rain barrel that caught the rain off the roof at the front corner of the house. They had an icebox, but ice delivery was apparently not always reliable in Gallup in those days.

Piñon Fudge

One of our favorite treats as children was fudge, made the old-fashioned way without marshmallow creams and all that. We used the recipe on the old cocoa cans. A new twist, however, is to add piñon nuts, which New Mexico kids gather easily in the fall from all the piñon trees on hillsides and mesas almost everywhere in the state. Piñon nuts are now fairly easy to find in health food and specialty stores thousands of miles from New Mexico. Piñon fudge is wonderful. Chop a half cup or so of nuts and add them to your favorite recipe!

Rellenos *(Manita style)*

This is a distinct northern New Mexican recipe, *pura manita*. It seems that very few Hispanics, except manitos, have ever heard of rellenos made this way. As with all regional foods, there are family variations, but this is the exact recipe Grandma Flora always used, right down to the baked red potato. Since she only made these rellenitos at Christmas time, it was something very special that we all looked forward to. Developing the knack to make them is worth the effort.

Serves 8

INGREDIENTS:

1/2 pound each of lean ground round and pork

1/2 cup shelled piñon nuts

1/2 cup raisins, chopped fine

1 small red potato, baked soft, cooled, peeled, and mashed

1/2 cup hot green chile, roasted, peeled, seeded, and chopped
    very small but not fine

1 egg, beaten

1/2 cup flour

1/2 teaspoon salt

enough cooking oil to keep the meatballs covered while frying

DIRECTIONS:

Combine the ground meat, piñon nuts, raisins, potato, and chile. Roll the mixture into round balls, about the size of golf balls. Dip the meatballs into the beaten egg to coat, roll them in salted flour, and then fry them in medium hot oil. Turn them carefully until cooked through on all sides, about 15 minutes. Drain them on paper towels. Grandma Flora served these as a special holiday dessert along with empanadas and coffee or eggnog.

Arroz Dulce *(Rice Pudding)*

Serves 8

INGREDIENTS:

1 cup short-grain rice

6 cups fresh whole milk

1 teaspoon salt

3/4 cup sugar

2 tablespoons butter

2 eggs, separated

1 tablespoon vanilla

1 teaspoon cinnamon

1/2 cup raisins, plumped and drained

DIRECTIONS:

Cook the rice in the milk in a double boiler for about 20-30 minutes until tender. Stir frequently and be sure it doesn't scorch. Stir in 1/2 cup of the sugar and the salt. Remove 1/2 cup of cooked milk and blend thoroughly into the egg yolks. Combine the blended yolks with the cooked rice. Add the butter, raisins, and vanilla and continue to cook for approximately 5 minutes. Beat the egg whites into soft peaks, gradually adding the remaining 1/2 cup of sugar. Fold the whites gently into the rice and dust the mixture with cinnamon. Serve warm or store it in the refrigerator and serve chilled.

Sopa

This dessert is also known to Spanish-speakers as *capirotada*, but northern New Mexicans always called it sopa. Grandma Flora prepared it fairly often, especially during Lent.

Serves 6

INGREDIENTS:

Pudding:

1 loaf of sliced, buttered, and oven-toasted French bread

1 cup raisins

$1/2$ cup piñon nuts

1 cup grated longhorn cheese

whipped cream

Sauce:

1 cup evaporated milk

1 cup water

2 teaspoons cinnamon

2 cups brown sugar

2 tablespoons butter

DIRECTIONS:

Preheat oven to 400 degrees.

Combine all the sauce ingredients. Heat to boiling and cook, stirring constantly for 3 minutes, and then set aside. Break the toasted bread into approximately 1-inch squares. Place one fourth of the bread, followed by one fourth of the raisins, cheese, and nuts into a buttered casserole dish. Pour one fourth of the sauce carefully over the top of the bread mixture, being sure to cover evenly. Repeat in layers until all the ingredients are used. Bake in a preheated 400-degree oven for 10 minutes. Serve topped with whipped cream and a sprinkle of cinnamon.

Flan

Serves 6

INGREDIENTS:

Syrup:

1¹/2 cups sugar

1 cup boiling water

Custard:

1 quart scalded milk

8 tablespoons sugar

1 teaspoon vanilla

6 whole eggs

1 cinnamon stick

dash of salt

DIRECTIONS:

Butter 6 custard cups. Preheat oven to 350 degrees.

Syrup: Melt the sugar in a heavy saucepan on low heat, stirring constantly, until it caramelizes into a golden brown. Continue stirring while you gradually add the water until you have a thin syrupy caramel. Allow it to cool slightly and then put two tablespoons of this caramel into each cup.

Custard: Scald the milk in a saucepan with a stick of cinnamon. While the milk is cooling, beat the eggs thoroughly until foamy in a large mixing bowl while gradually adding the sugar. Add the vanilla and then blend in the milk mixture, stirring constantly. Pour the mixture into the custard cups and put the cups into a large baking pan, approximately 13x9x2 inches. Pour very hot water carefully into the baking pan up to 1/2 inch from the tops of the custard cups.

Bake at 350 degrees for about 45 minutes or until custard is set. Test for doneness by inserting a knife into the custard: if it comes out clean, it's done. Remove your custard cups from the oven and cool. If you wish to serve the custard unmolded, run a sharp knife along the edge of each cup and dip the bottom into hot water. Invert each cup onto a dessert dish and top the custard with whipped cream to serve.

Empanaditas

These "little turnovers" are a delicacy similar to European turnovers and appear in numerous versions in New Mexico. In fact, this was a difficult recipe to duplicate in exactly the same way that Grandma Flora made it because she used it in so many different forms. Our favorite version is pumpkin, the recipe included here, but any kind of fruit or minced-meat filling can be used. (You will also see these turnovers referred to simply as empanadas.)

INGREDIENTS:

Filling:

1 1/2 cups canned pumpkin

3/4 cup sugar

1/2 teaspoon salt

1 teaspoon cinnamon

1 teaspoon nutmeg

1/2 teaspoon ground cloves

3 slightly beaten eggs

1 13-ounce can evaporated milk

Dough:

(You may want to use your own favorite pastry recipe.)

4 cups flour

1 teaspoon baking powder

1 teaspoon salt

1 1/2 cups shortening (any good low-cholesterol brand)

8-10 tablespoons ice water

DIRECTIONS:

Preheat oven to 350 degrees. Combine all the filling ingredients in a large mixing bowl and set it aside while you make the pastry.

If you want to follow Grandma Flora's dough recipe: sift together the flour, baking powder, and salt. Cut in the shortening and mix well. Add the ice water until the dough is moist and pliable but not sticky. Grandma Flora's empanaditas had a rather thick substantial pastry, rather than the very light version we have sometimes tried.

Roll out the dough on a floured surface. Cut the dough into 5-inch rounds with the lid of a large coffee can, or something similar, to maintain consistency. Spoon 3 tablespoons of the filling into the center of each round and fold it in half, sealing the edges firmly and evenly.

Place the empanaditas on a baking sheet and bake in a preheated 350-degree oven for 15 to 20 minutes or until lightly browned.

Natillas

Natillas is the name for a delicate egg custard with a meringue gently folded into it and a light dusting of freshly grated nutmeg and cinnamon. This delicious dessert was also served as a delightful breakfast or a soothing remedio for someone too sick to have a heavy meal.

Serves 6-8

INGREDIENTS:

4 egg yolks

2 tablespoons corn starch

dash of salt

2$^{1}/_{2}$ cups fresh milk

1 teaspoon vanilla

4 egg whites

2 tablespoons sugar
nutmeg
cinnamon

DIRECTIONS:

Thoroughly combine the egg yolks, corn starch, salt, and $^1/_2$ cup of sugar in a medium saucepan. Add the milk and vanilla and cook over medium heat, stirring constantly, until the mixture has thickened to the consistency of custard. Remove the pan from the heat and set aside. Beat the egg whites into soft peaks and gradually add the remaining $^1/_2$ cup of sugar.

When the custard mixture has cooled, gently fold in the egg whites and sprinkle the freshly grated nutmeg and cinnamon on top. Natillas can be served immediately or chilled briefly, but it does not keep for very long.

Biscochitos

The very ultimate in manito confections are the biscochitos. They are essential to many manito family holidays, usually making their appearance right after Thanksgiving to be shared as gifts for favorite people or stored away for holiday parties later. I can think of very few Christmas gifts that are more appealing than a basket of these subtly flavored cookies.

Some people prefer biscochitos barely sweet. The recipe I include here produces a medium to light sweetness, so you can taste the anise a little more. Some biscochito afficionados prefer a crispy, thinly rolled bisco. Others prefer them a bit thick and soft. This recipe should produce a fragrant, delicate, slightly crispy cookie.

Makes 6 dozen cookies

INGREDIENTS:

6-8 cups all-purpose flour

5 teaspoons baking powder

pinch of salt

1 3/4 cups white sugar

1 cup brown sugar

2 cups melted Crisco or lard

4 eggs

1 cup milk

2 teaspoons anise seeds

3/4 cup water

2 1/2 teaspoons cinnamon

DIRECTIONS:

Preheat the oven to 350 degrees.

Sift 6 cups of the flour with the baking powder and salt and set it aside. Cream together 1 1/2 cups of white sugar and 1 cup of brown sugar with the shortening. Add the eggs and milk and mix well. Meanwhile simmer the anise in 3/4 cup water and then stir it into the sugar, shortening, and egg mixture. Gradually add the sifted flour mixture.

Prepare your rolling surface and pastry rolling pin with a light dusting of flour. (Grandma Flora always used a sifter.) Be careful because too much flour will toughen the dough. Add additional flour gradually just until the dough binds together and no longer sticks easily to the rolling surface. Roll out the dough to approximately 1/4-inch thick and cut with a cookie cutter. I find that a 3-inch size is best and let the shape be dictated by the occasion. Easter eggs are just as welcome as hearts or stars, depending on the season.

Dust the cookies with a mixture of 1 part cinnamon to 2 parts sugar. Transfer them to a cookie sheet and bake for about 10 minutes. Watch them carefully and be ready to remove them when they reach an even, delicate brown.

Pastelitos

I'm not sure why, but we saw this dish more often in other people's homes than our own. If you can handle pastry, it's very easy to make. Grandma Flora used dried fruit to make it. We speculate that because she usually preserved rather than dried fruits, perhaps simple availability was why we didn't have pastelitos as often as our neighbors. In any case, they are a very popular traditional Nuevo Mexico treat, especially for the winter holidays. I use a 10x14-inch cookie sheet to bake them.

Makes about 30 2-inch squares

INGREDIENTS:

Filling:

3 cups dried fruit of choice (apricots and apples were often used)

3/4 cup sugar

1/2 cup water

1 tablespoon lemon juice

1 teaspoon freshly grated nutmeg

1 teaspoon freshly grated cinnamon

Pastry:

2 cups all purpose flour

1 tablespoon sugar

1 teaspoon baking powder

1/2 teaspoon salt

2/3 cup shortening

1/2 cup milk

cinnamon and sugar mixture (approximately 4 tablespoons of sugar mixed
  with 2 teaspoons of cinnamon)

DIRECTIONS:

Combine the fruit with all other filling ingredients in a saucepan and cook over medium heat until the mix thickens to the consistency of a thick syrup. Allow it to cool.

Preheat the oven to 400 degrees. Combine the flour, sugar, baking powder, and salt in a mixing bowl. Cut in the shortening with a couple of knives or pastry blender until the mixture is crumbly. Gradually add the milk and mix until evenly moist. Knead the dough gently until it's easy to handle.

Roll out half of the dough on a lightly floured surface to about $1/8$ of an inch thick and 10x14 inches in size. Fold the dough in half to lift and fit it onto a 10x14 cookie sheet (the kind with sides). Spread the cooled filling onto the dough. Roll out the rest of the dough as before and place over the fruit. Trim and decorate the edges of the pastry dough and sprinkle with the mixture of sugar and cinnamon. A salt shaker works well for distributing it evenly over the large surface. Prick the top of the pastry as you would for a pie and bake at 400 degrees until lightly browned, about 15 minutes. When it has fully cooled, cut the pastelitos into squares.

Raisin Walnut Bars

Grandma Flora loved to bake and seemed to enjoy indulging her sweet tooth. She preserved any kind of fruit available and often used the preserves in baking. She also favored orange peel in sweets. Here is one of our favorites.

Fills an 8-inch square pan and makes about 16 2-inch squares

INGREDIENTS:

Filling:

1 cup chopped raisins

$1/2$ cup plum jam

2 eggs

3/4 cup packed brown sugar

1/2 cup all-purpose flour

1/2 teaspoon baking powder

1/2 teaspoon salt

1 cup chopped nuts (walnuts work well)

1 teaspoon orange peel

1 teaspoon vanilla

powdered sugar

Shortbread:

1^1/2 cups all-purpose flour

1/2 cup butter

1/3 cup sugar

D IRECTIONS:

Preheat oven to 350 degrees. Combine the shortbread ingredients. Press the mixture firmly into the bottom of a greased 8-inch square pan. Bake at 350 degrees until the edges are lightly browned, usually about 25 minutes.

Mix the raisins and jam and set aside. Combine the flour, baking powder, and salt in a medium-sized bowl. Beat the eggs into the brown sugar separately and then blend the mixture into the dry ingredients. Add the walnuts, orange peel, and vanilla. Spread the entire mixture over the shortbread base and return it to the oven. Bake for 35 minutes or until the top is browned and springs back at the touch. Cool completely and then cut into bars as large or small as you like.

Walnut Orange Bread

Makes one loaf

INGREDIENTS:

3 cups all-purpose flour

3/4 cup sugar

2 teaspoons baking powder

1/2 teaspoon salt

1 egg, lightly beaten

1/2 cup melted butter

1 cup milk

1/2 cup fresh squeezed orange juice

1 teaspoon grated orange peel

1 cup chopped walnuts

DIRECTIONS:

Grease a 9x5x3-inch loaf pan. Preheat oven to 350 degrees. Combine the sugar, baking powder, and salt. Add the egg, melted butter, milk, and orange peel. Mix until all of the mixture is moistened and then stir in the walnuts. Pour it into a greased loaf pan and bake at 350 degrees for one hour or until a toothpick or knife inserted in the center of the loaf comes out clean. Let it set for 15 minutes and then turn the loaf out onto a wire rack to cool fully before slicing.

Zucchini and Orange Bread

Makes 2 loaves

INGREDIENTS:

3 eggs, slightly beaten

1 cup oil

2 cups sugar

3 teaspoons vanilla

2 cups grated zucchini

$^1/_2$ cup shredded orange peel

3 cups all-purpose flour

1 teaspoon salt

$^1/_2$ teaspoon baking soda

1 teaspoon baking powder

3 teaspoons ground cinnamon

$^1/_2$ cup coarsely chopped nuts

$^1/_2$ cup raisins

DIRECTIONS:

Grease and flour two 9x5x3-inch loaf pans. Preheat the oven to 350 degrees.

Gently blend the eggs and oil into the sugar. Add the zucchini, orange peel, and vanilla. Combine the flour, salt, baking powder, baking soda, and cinnamon separately. Then add the wet mixture to the dry, being careful not to overmix. Blend the nuts and raisins gently into the batter with a fork to distribute evenly. Pour the batter into the prepared loaf pans and bake at 350 degrees for 1 hour. Immediately turn the loaves out onto racks to cool.

Fruit Cocktail Cake

Grandma and everyone else we knew had pantries well stocked with canned fruit to satisfy winter cravings. Sometimes we ate chilled canned peaches just as they came from the can or Jell-O with fruit cocktail or bananas. But this cake recipe was something a little special.

INGREDIENTS:

$1^1/_2$ cup sugar

2 cups flour

$^1/_2$ cup melted butter

2 beaten eggs

1 #303 can fruit cocktail with juice

1 teaspoon baking soda

$1/2$ teaspoon salt

1 teaspoon vanilla extract

DIRECTIONS:

Mix all the ingredients in a large mixing bowl in the order given. Stir well and pour into a well-greased and floured 9x13-inch baking pan. Bake in a pre-heated 300-degree oven for 1 hour. After baking, prepare the icing.

Icing

INGREDIENTS:

1 13-ounce can evaporated milk

$3/4$ cup sugar

whipped cream

DIRECTIONS:

Mix the milk and sugar in a small saucepan and cook to the "soft ball" stage. (Test by dropping a few drops into a cup of water and seeing if it forms a soft ball.) Evenly perforate the baked cake surface with a fork and then pour the icing mixture evenly over the cake. Serve warm, topped with a dollop of whipped cream.

Chapter 8

¿Quién Sabe En Qué Palo Irá A Parar La Paloma?

ONE NEVER KNOWS ON WHICH BRANCH THE BIRD WILL ALIGHT

Don Lorenzo Hubbell, Melitón's uncle,
probably around 1900 when he was
a Territorial Representative

(COURTESY OF THE ARIZONA HISTORICAL SOCIETY, #15802)

My father, Antonio Arturo Romero, was the oldest son, a position of responsibility in Hispanic families. After his father died in 1932, he became a sort of substitute father to the youngest children until he married our mother a few years later. His older sisters, Carlotta, Jenny, and Flora, were already married. They had grown up during the Roaring Twenties and had developed a spirit of independence uncommon in the manito community of their parents.

Carlotta, the oldest, had married and moved to Santa Fe, where she and her husband owned a grocery store. She was still very young when widowed. In the late thirties she went to work for the federal government. Jenny (or Juana, as my father usually called her) was the second eldest sister; she married, divorced, and eventually married again. Flora, nicknamed Lala, married a man who had traded the Dust Bowl of Oklahoma for the business opportunities of New Mexico. Together they ran Shorty's Electric Shop in Gallup.

The author's father,
Antonio Romero, at four years old

My uncle Melquiades, the second son, was born in 1915 shortly before the family moved to Gallup. He was left in Albuquerque as a gift child to Grandma Flora's sister Carmelita, who never had children of her own. Then came Uncle Fernando, born in Gallup in 1918. Following Nando were our Uncle Román and Uncle Tito. Uncle Tito was christened Andrés but was such a beautiful child that Grandma called him *"Santito,"* Little Saint. He served in the Navy, then married and lived in

the house next to Grandma's, one that my father helped to build. Aunt Lupe was next and became another gift child, raised by Grandpa Melitón's childless sister, Amelia. Then came Mary, followed by Dolores, the youngest.

With the exception of her first child, Carlotta, who was born with the help of a midwife, all of Grandma Flora's children were born at home with only her oldest daughters to help. And the only help they gave was with preparations for the delivery and then washing the baby their mother had delivered sola to be shown to the family shortly after. She was truly a pioneer woman.

In the mid twenties, Grandpa Melitón took the family to live on the Navajo Reservation. At first they lived at their uncle Lorenzo Hubbell's Ganado trading post, which is now a national historic site. (Doña Lina had died in 1913, but true to Hispanic traditions, Don Lorenzo maintained close contacts with his wife's relatives until he died.) I like to go to the Hubbell Trading Post still and see the old screened porch where my father slept in the summer time as a child. He worked at the post for his great uncle (and Lorenzo's son Roman) and remembered the renowned don very well. He often said that you could set your clock by Uncle Lorenzo's industrious activities. The old man did his paperwork in his office until midnight, when the light would go off without fail. Then he would be up again at four o'clock in the morning tending to the chores. As an employee at the post, my father had to learn Navajo, on top of his Spanish and English, to be able to speak with the customers.

Later in the decade, Melitón and Flora moved further north to Round Rock to run the trading post there. Four children were still with them: Fernando, Román, Mary, and Dolores. Life was much different for the

The Hubbell Trading Post at Ganado on the Navajo Reservation, probably around the 1890s. The family residence is behind the trading post. (COURTESY OF THE ARIZONA HISTORICAL SOCIETY, #48631)

family out in this more remote part of the reservation, according to our Aunt Dolores. The boys were older and could be left on their own when not working in the trading post. But the girls were still toddlers, so Grandpa took two dogs with them, a boxer for Mary and a German shepherd for Dolores. Dolores was sickly and Grandpa believed that she had tuberculosis. Staying outdoors in the sun was the prescribed cure for TB at the time, so little Lolie was allowed to stay in the sun as much as possible with the German shepherd as her nanny.

At first the Navajo people from around the Round Rock area did not welcome the Romeros, mainly because of unfortunate experiences with earlier traders. (Many of those Navajo still vividly recalled the horror of the Long Walk to Fort Sumner and Bosque Redondo.) My grandparents respected the culture and religion of the people of Round Rock, however; and because Melitón and Flora retained their own dignity, values, and identity, they were respected in turn. Later the Navajo around Round Rock also came to respect my Grandma Flora for her talents as a healer.

Apparently it all started with a Navajo woman who became ill after eating overripe peaches. Grandma Flora automatically went to work and brewed a healing tea for her from a yerba she knew. Shortly after that, Flora cured a man of some persistent sores on his hand. Soon people were coming in droves, and the trading post often looked like a hospital with people lining up for help from Flora. After the family left the trading post, Grandpa liked to say that the Navajos who came to say goodbye told him that he could leave, but Grandma Flora should stay. Eventually, my grandfather's younger brother Claudio owned and operated that remote post until the 1950s.

It was after they had been at Round Rock for two or three years that Dolores contracted typhoid fever and Grandpa Melitón decided it was time to move the family back to Gallup. Typhoid was so deadly that he thought their fragile child would probably not survive, and he wanted her to be in their own home when she died. Several times her breathing was too shallow to detect, and Grandpa sadly covered her up and told Grandma that she had died. Each time, Grandma uncovered her to find that she was still alive and continued her attempts to nurse her back to health. And once again, her healing skills were successful.

About 1931, Grandpa Melitón suffered a stroke that paralyzed his right side. He never recovered. While he was bedridden, he often had little Dolores, who by then had recovered from typhoid, bring her toys to the big iron bed so he could watch over her. She recalls that one day while she was playing there was suddenly a lot of activity around the bed. She became frightened, crawled under the bed, and then saw her father's huge forearm fall to the side of the bed. She realized later that must have been the moment that he died.

His death was in the summer of 1932, during the Great Depression.

The inside of the Hubbell warehouse was typical of most trading posts of the times. Lorenzo Hubbell is seated on the wool sacks at left. (Courtesy of the Museum of New Mexico, #16037)

At the time, our father was working in the CCC Camp in Oregon and was unable to raise enough money in time to get back to New Mexico for the funeral. When he came home, he took on the responsibility of helping to support his younger brothers and sisters.

Melitón and Flora's family underwent even more changes during the tumultuous years of World War II. At the age of fifteen, Dolores went into the convent of the Poor Sisters of Saint Francis of Perpetual Adoration, where she became a nurse. She insists that her mother, Grandma Flora, did not impose her own wish to become a nun onto her youngest daughter. Dolores maintains that although she was impressed by her mother's devotion, she was motivated by the peace and satisfaction she herself had seen in the nuns at their schools. She ended up leaving the convent, however,

and marrying. She now lives in Kirkland, Washington, near Seattle after raising seven children. My parents (Antonio and Benina) went to Richmond, California, to work in the shipyards during the war. They had three children at the time: my sister Lorease, my brother Loriboy (whose given name is Lorenzo after Uncle Lorenzo), and Marsha. Aunt Mary, who was still just a teenager, went with them. They were all making more money than any of them had ever made before and were so unaccustomed to having money that they kept it in shoeboxes in the closet.

Uncle Mel and his wife moved to Los Angeles and raised their two children there. Uncle Fernando moved over to the Flagstaff area during the forties, raised four children, and lives there still. Aunt Lala stayed in Gallup until she and her husband moved into a retirement community in Arizona. Aunt Lupe (raised by Melitón's sister Amelia) and her husband settled here in Albuquerque, after many years of traveling in military service.

Grandma Flora stayed in the adobe house at the corner of Wilson and 8th Streets in the old northside of Gallup with Uncle Román after he came home from Europe. (Across the street was the Hubbell's old family home.) Eventually, Carlotta (Dad's oldest sister) moved to Seattle, followed by Jenny and Mary and their husbands. In 1948, Carlotta convinced my father that Seattle offered good opportunities for our growing family, too. Off we went to Seattle for my father to work at Boeing Aircraft for two years.

Then when my father and mother brought us back to Gallup from Richmond, we lived in the old house and Grandma and Román moved to the smaller house nearby. (By this time there were two more little Romeros—me and my younger brother, Tim.) We played a sort of musical chairs with the two houses as my father moved us back and forth between the West Coast and New Mexico, according to working conditions.

After Uncle Román died in 1950, Grandma Flora left Gallup and joined Carlotta, Jenny, and Mary in Seattle, around the time that my father moved us back to New Mexico. (He took us on another round to the Northwest two years later before we came back again in 1955.)

Grandma stayed in Seattle for the last years of her life, living with Carlotta and helping to care for her many grandchildren. She was far from the dusty mesas of New Mexico, but she retained her traditions and the grace of spirit so typical of New Mexico's manitos. Until her last years, she prepared most of the meals for her daughters' families. The kitchen at Carlotta's apartment was her domain. Her Sunday dinners were as good as ever, even in that tiny little apartment. And the high points of our outings to Green Lake and Madrona Beach were the wonderful picnic lunches that Grandma made for us.

Five years ago, I moved back to Albuquerque with my youngest son to get back in touch *con mis antepasados.* It seems as though all those family stories that I had listened to so eagerly had drawn me back to their source, to the herencia from Grandma Flora. My little "Gramacita" lives on through my three children and their children, still teaching her family through the ideals she taught to my father and to me. And perhaps as a legacy of Grandma Flora's interest and talent in healing, several of Grandma Flora's grandchildren eventually took up careers in medicine, including my oldest son John. Time will tell what my youngest son Dominic will choose.

Flora Durán Romero was far more than a gourmet cook—she was strongest in her gentle response to a world filled with danger, pain, and unpredictability and in her constant awareness of the blessings we are all given to enjoy. Flora lived her faith daily until she died in Seattle in 1966,

the same year that my daughter, Tracy, was born. She was a true pioneer woman, accepting her fate in this world willingly and remaining content in spite of the hardships she suffered.

Both my grandmother and my father remain, to me, representatives of the old manito community that gave birth to us all: responsible, industrious, and truly unmaterialistic. They both believed in the innate goodness of all children and the infinite power of prayer and faith in God. Antonio seemed to share little of his fiery father's personality traits; he was a quiet, introspective man and his life emulated his mother's. They were both infinitely kind and charitable, strict in the teachings to care for children and the elderly and that family always comes first. Of all the old dichos, the one that suits my father and his mother best is, *"Cuándo uno es mas pobre, se le debe socorrer mas."* To one who needs the most, give the most.

Glossary

abuela / abuelo: grandmother, grandfather

antepasados: ancestors, forefathers

aperitivos: appetizers

bandejita: in New Mexico, a pan or basin

bautismo: baptism, of newborn babies in this case

biscochitos / bizcochitos: traditional New Mexican cookies, spelled both
  ways but usually the former in northern New Mexico

caldo: in New Mexico, a stew

chile / chili: chile refers to the actual plant and its fiery fruit; chili is the
  dish of meat and beans spiced with chile that was popularized in Texas
  as a barbecue entrée

colchone: handmade wool mattress

comal: stovetop lid

comida sabrosa: delicious food

compadres: in a literal sense, godparents; but in a general sense, families
  closely linked by either blood, marriage, or other special circumstances

creencia: belief

cuaresmale: food prepared especially during the Lenten season

dicho: saying or proverb

Él sonrió y se fue: he smiled and left

empanadas / empanaditas: turnovers, little turnovers

Es un sombrero para un toro: it's a hat for a bull

Eso es todo lo que tienes que saber: that is all that you need to know

fideos: noodles, especially fine thin noodles such as vermicelli

flautas: literally "flutes;" in relation to food, small tortillas rolled up around
  a filling and fried

grano: (slang) a craving for something

güeritos: small, round yellow chile peppers, usually quite hot

habanero: especially hot chiles originally from the Caribbean

herencia: heritage

hermanitos / manitos: little brothers

hijados: godchildren

hoja: corn husk

horno: oven

lana: wool

metate: stone grinding surface, usually with a shallow curved shape

molcajete: stone grinding bowl, mortar

muy picante: very spicy

nixtamal: uncooked hominy

no bueno por nada: good for nothing

no llores, mijita: don't cry, my dear little daughter

padrinos: godparents

pellejo: skin

Plaza Vieja: the Old Plaza

La práctica hace una maestra: practice makes the master (practice makes
  perfect)

prendorio: engagement ceremony

pueblo / Pueblo: town or village; when capitalized, Pueblo refers to the
  Indian peoples who settled in villages along or not far from the Río
  Grande in pre-Columbian times

quelites: leafy greens from amaranth, lamb's quarters, and other similar
  plants

queso asadero: a Mexican cheese common in New Mexico, Arizona, and
  Texas

remedios: remedies, cures

ristra: strands of chiles tied onto lengths of twine to dry

salvo: a toast

sola: alone

tío / tía: uncle, aunt

tocayo: namesake

vecino: neighbor

velorio: funeral

yerba (also spelled hierba): grass or herb; in New Mexico it also refers
  to a tea

Notes

Notes

Notes

Notes

Notes

Notes

Notes